A SPIRITUAL
UNDERSTANDING
OF LIFE

Barry Lee

authorHOUSE®

AuthorHouse™ UK Ltd.
500 Avebury Boulevard
Central Milton Keynes, MK9 2BE
www.authorhouse.co.uk
Phone: 08001974150

First published by AuthorHouse 1/29/2011

ISBN: 978-1-4567-7038-9

This book is printed on acid-free paper.

To Jaqi

one of the most spiritual people
whom I have known

Contents

Preface/Introduction

I think of myself as a 'spiritual' person who can recognise the attributes of spirituality in other people. This book is an attempt to explain, hopefully in simple terms, what I mean by 'spiritual' and to suggest how spiritual people operate. It is aimed at people with an interest in spiritual matters, whether in the context of faith or through some other life experience. As it happens, I express my spirituality through being a Christian (though some Christians would find this book unacceptable as an interpretation of the Christian way because there are many features of institutional Christianity which I cannot endorse). I do not expect all people to express their spirituality through Christianity or any other religion, nor do I think that any religion should claim to be the only way to knowledge, truth and freedom. Indeed, in my life I have been close to many people who have no religious faith (indeed in some cases are hostile to the idea of religion because of its negative impact on the world) and found them truly spiritual and more "Christian" in my eyes than some who claim to be Christian. Similarly, I have had friendships with people of faiths other than Christianity and found them to be deeply spiritual. Thus I am not using this book to promote Christianity; I will, however, in the final chapter, say something about the features of Christianity which I hold dear and which enable me to express my spirituality.

I should also state at the beginning that I am one of the more fortunate people in this world because I live in one of the wealthiest countries. As a result my perspectives are those of a white, male, educated, middle-age, middle-class European, and, though I try hard to broaden my understanding of the lives of other people, inevitably the book has emerged from this background with many flaws for which I can only apologise to the reader.

The book is organised into three parts in twelve chapters. The first part explores the background ideas and five chapters express my discoveries about, and experience of, spirituality in terms of how the spirit manifests itself, the role of the soul and what we can learn from religions. The second part examines practical dimensions of spiritual living, with six chapters on connectedness, ethics, creativity, speaking about spirituality, prayer, and living with pain, suffering and death. The third part in a single chapter discusses Christianity as my vehicle for spiritual living. An Appendix provides more detail about the religions mentioned in the book.

If you are more interested in the practical consequences of the spiritual understanding of life than in the arguments about where spirituality comes from and how it works, then chapter 4 on feeding the soul followed by chapters 6 to 11 would be a good way-in; you can always come back to the others later!

In order to facilitate small group discussion of the book there are at the end of each chapter a number of points for consideration in discussion. These could equally well be points for reflection for individuals on reaching the end of each chapter. The final pages offers some guidance on follow-up materials.

I have called the book "A spiritual understanding of life" because I want to contrast it with the material understanding of life which has come to dominate the world as I have experienced it. Another title could have been "The spirit sets us free" because I believe that living in tune with the spirit keeps human beings free to fulfil their potential, which is the purpose of our life on earth, and free from the propaganda of religion, politics, economics, violence and the media which seek to dominate our lives.

PART 1

Background on spirituality, the soul and religion

1. A Spiritual Understanding of Life

In the past 100 years, and especially the past 50 which constitute the bulk of my time on earth, for many human beings their understanding of life has significantly changed, especially in the western world, from being more spiritually based to being more materially based. Spirituality and materialism are at opposite ends of a spectrum of ways of viewing our existence. Let me present a picture of the extremes and you can see whether you agree with me that the movement has been away from the spiritual and towards the materialist end of the spectrum. Clearly people will locate themselves at points along the spectrum rather than at the extremes, but the spectrum helps us to decide whether there has been a change.

A materialist outlook

Here are some adjectives or phrases that could be used to describe a materialist outlook on life: consumerist and focused on material things/possessions; short-term and instrumental; inward-looking and self-interested; individualistic; superficial and shallow; seeing the worst in people and being dismissive of them; a 'couldn't care less' attitude.

In the west we live in a world which is largely dominated by the consumption of material things. Indeed the recent credit crunch in 2008 was the consequence of a frenzy of consuming. Certain economists taught that growth in economic wealth would best be fuelled by production of more and cheaper things for people to buy and that purchasing should be fuelled by the provision of easy credit. So people (and countries) became more and more in debt and those funding the debts took greater and greater risks until the point was reached when the so-called toxicity of the debts (i.e. their unrealistic foundation) caused much of the banking system to collapse and seek state underpinning. Many western economies were living beyond their means and had encouraged their people to do the same. The mass media were used to stimulate consumption by people who could not afford the items which they were urged to acquire. The methods of stimulation moved on from simply providing information about products to using so-called 'product placement' to convince people that they could not live without the items on display. The acquisitiveness which may be innate in human nature was greatly inflamed by deliberate manipulation ("hidden persuasion") using the mass media.

You might at this point be saying to yourself that people do not have to fall for the blandishments of the marketing messages and you would be right if it were not for the fact that ordinary people are surrounded at all times and in all places by aggressive, albeit subtle, suggestions that fulfilment in life is to be measured by quantity of possessions. This is consumerism for its own sake and it has become a major feature of the media who draw their income from advertising, including commercial television and radio, newspapers, magazines and the internet. These channels have become so widespread and so intimate over the past 30-50 years that they have created a new cultural form based almost entirely on materialism.

I believe that one consequence of such manipulation of our lives and thoughts is the distancing of people from one another, a break-down of the cohesion which enabled society to function effectively. More and more people live in a make-believe world in which consuming is all important and previously held values about the importance of honesty, trust and caring for one another are losing importance. Such is the impact of the make-believe world that for some people, when they come across an issue or an event that disturbs them, they do not know whether it is real and whether they can do anything about it. As a result they have feelings of both depersonalisation (everything around them is fabricated and false) and alienation from the real things that happen from day-to-day.

Two very different examples of this are the development of reality television and the exploitative portrayal of violence on our television screens. The development of so-called reality television, which is artificial, false and manipulated, has had the effect of disabling the discernment of some television viewers, who may become less and less able to distinguish truth from falsehood; some daytime television shows build on this by encouraging people to tell lies in order to win prizes. The portrayal of violence on our television screens and in films is particularly exploitative; it exploits the people involved, especially if it is based on real events, and it exploits the viewer because the scenes are rarely placed in context, rarely explained and presented as the norm; many are convinced that levels of violence and crime have increased in our streets because they are glamourised by the media. It is disheartening that when challenged the presenters use the excuse of people 'needing to know' when they broadcast show after show of freakish events that are presented as though they are the norm when in practice they are completely exceptional. They set out to titivate and seem to have no sense of responsibility for the outcomes.

Three other related features of the way the media impact on the consumerist societies in which we live are celebrities, chat shows and absence of news. The various media seem to fill their channels with self-generated material that often bears no resemblance to the real world. They find individuals who are willing to be turned into celebrities and they re-invent them in order to fill and sell their programmes and publications. The willingness of the so-called celebrities to be manipulated in the way that they are is sad, an indicator of the artificial world in which many people now seem to live. Competition among the mass media has led to a need to cut costs and one solution has been to create celebrities who appear on low cost chat shows or reality television programmes, reinforced by popular magazines. This is manufactured entertainment which is cheap in more senses than one. Sadly it has carried through into some news programmes and news papers which seem to have less concern to provide news than to provide vehicles for the promotion of the views of chosen individuals. It is no surprise that so many people have little feel for what is really happening in the world and increasingly feel distanced from it.

This rather strong attack on the media's contribution to the development of a consumerist outlook is, of course, a picture of one extreme. There are compensating factors such as the greater choice of media channels than ever before, the huge increase in the use of personal technology (mobile phone, computer, internet, social networks etc.), the ways in which people can contribute their ideas and experiences through blogs, twitters, submission of news reports by mobile phone, and the very rapid sharing of news as a result of advances in communications technology. There are also many wonderful, informative programmes on radio and television that can be spiritually uplifting.

The materialist outlook on life leads to feelings of envy and greed which, if allowed to dominate the personality, cause the individual to lose sight of other important aspects of life. It promotes instant gratification – people are encouraged not only to want things but to want them now. There is less willingness to wait, to save and to spend time evaluating whether the object wanted has real worth. People have been encouraged to focus on the short term and the easy availability of credit has facilitated such attitudes. In turn short-term thinking leads to a throw-away mode of life in which products are replaced much earlier than is really necessary and huge amounts of waste are the consequence.

One feature of consumerism is increased individualism. The way in which consumerism is promoted is through the idea of competition; the individual is persuaded to compete with others in his or her use of resources in order to be different. This individualism undermines ideas of collaboration which are at the root of all successful human endeavour. If people are encouraged only to compete, they miss out on the delights of working together and benefitting from the ideas of others. Similarly individualism leads to greater fragmentation of life and of society; if people operate largely alone or keep different parts of their lives separate, the outcome is a much less integrated and holistic approach to life. This, of course, is promoted by the producers of goods because they can persuade people to throw things away instead of holding on to them because they "need to have the latest fashions" to mark their position in society. Fashion no longer relates simply to clothes as it used to do; now it refers to any product from cars to bathroom suites, from hiking gear to cooking utensils, from perfumes to kitchen cleaners. The products in themselves are not greatly different but their packaging (both physical and psychological) is and people can be persuaded to waste resources by adopting a particular life-style which demands a certain look or style. This kind of individuality is shallow; it does not relate to how people think or work or care but to what they wear, the car they drive and the drinks they prefer.

Ironically whilst individualism is the target of the marketing departments, true individualism (i.e. the individual achieving his or her potential) is reducing; we increasingly are encouraged to belong to market segments which conform to certain media-driven norms. For example, you might be forgiven for thinking that all young male adolescents are binge-drinkers because this is presented as the sign of conformity to the notional group; sadly this ignores the many who are pursuing their gifts and talents in a creative way or enjoying the company of caring friends. In the desire to simplify and categorise, the individual is not allowed to be different; and there is enormous commercial pressure on people to do the group things, drink the group drinks and be part of the group behaviour.

For others the emphasis on individualism takes a different form. They turn in on themselves and lose the sense of being part of a community which used to be so important to people's lives. The television, the computer game and the internet do not require interaction with others. It is possible to lock oneself away and become introspective and inward-looking, believing that you are finding some fulfilment in life without other people. Of course, nothing could be further from the truth than the idea that it is possible to live a full human life without the company and pleasure of others. There is no doubt that losing oneself in a novel or a game or a television programme can be absorbing and pleasurable but usually in the context of sharing one's delight with others.

A major consequence of these changes is that many people are becoming more self-interested and self-centred. They have less interest in others and their needs. They are encouraged to look for short-term personal pleasure, sometimes at the expense of others. They are taught by the developing cultural norm to seek to dominate other people rather than co-operate with them. They move in circles which are increasingly exclusive rather than inclusive, almost closed societies which have led governments to be very concerned about social cohesion. Such closed societies inevitably become rigid and conservative in outlook, seeking to preserve their own model of living and impervious to the good ideas from others. They tend to place constraints on their members who surrender their freedom of thought to some idea of an exclusive better way of life. This leads to fear, criticism and even contempt of those who are different. They can be dismissive of the values of other groups, seeing the worst in them rather than the best. Eventually they can lose compassion for those around them and couldn't care less about their situation. Such is the road to fascism and conflict.

Some would argue that the self-centred, materialist understanding of life is the natural outlook for the human being, almost hard-wired into the personality. If this is the case, they argue, the increase in materialism is inevitable and unsurprising. Certainly if we look at the way the western world has changed, even if you do not entirely agree with my analysis, we might be forgiven for thinking that power, greed, money, violence and worship of self have become the norm. However, my understanding of life and of what drives human beings is very different. All around me people are wanting the freedom (from manipulation, greed and short-term thinking) to base their values on a spiritual understanding of life in which hope, compassion, building and serving are the key notes. Such people are horrified that they are caught up in a culture of personal greed, dishonesty, waste, violence and overall lack of moral principles whilst surrounded day-by-day by global poverty and huge inequalities created by lack of access to fair trade, education, health, food and shelter. This applies in the developed world as well as, but not as severely as, in the developing world.

A spiritual outlook

At the other end of the spectrum is the spiritual outlook. Here are some adjectives or phrases that could be used to describe a spiritual outlook: long-term and outward looking; interested in others and collaborative; delighted by mystery and grateful; community- and people-focused; constructive and inclusive; transforming and confident; exploring but disciplined; attentive and wise.

A spiritual outlook on life starts with the other person, believing that our human existence is not spent alone and in isolation but is tied to all other human beings who are alive with us, have lived before and will live after us. Whilst a sense of self is important, the spiritual person makes sure that it does not lead to self-centred-ness. Life is lived through other people with whom we are in relationship (and vice versa). Thus the spiritual understanding of life looks towards the well-being of others before personal gain, and resists the social pressure towards self-aggrandisement when others, whether close at hand or far way, are suffering and have little that they can call their own.

Because the spiritual understanding of life looks to the past, present and future of the human race, it takes a long-term, even eternal, perspective; the short-term and instrumental is less important. Similarly the spiritual view tries to be holistic rather than fragmented or short-sighted; it attempts to see things in context and understands that all things and all people are in some way inter-related. Thus the impact of decisions about the use of time or money will be considered before they are made and every effort devoted to minimise negative effects on others.

The spiritual view is outward-looking and celebratory in its concern for others. It rejoices when others do well and it is compassionate when others are hurting and in distress. It does not seek to gain at others' expense; where it has seen success or wealth or good health or great friendship, it is generous towards others who have less. It sees service to others as its main motivating force. Its overall attitude is one of joy, looking for the best in people and seeking their personal growth. It never puts people down but seeks always to build them up. Thus its approach to others is caring, collaborative and cooperative rather than competitive and self-seeking. This results in an emphasis on community and cohesion.

In a person's dealing with people, the spiritual outlook is attentive, conscientious and caring. The spiritual person tries to be a person of wisdom to whom others can come for advice. This wisdom draws on spiritual depth but it is not rigid or fixed. The spiritual person is an explorer, progressive in viewpoint, always learning new things, open to new ideas and spontaneous. The inner discipline which is part of the spiritual understanding of life gives a strength and depth which is transformative both of people and of ideas.

Unlike the materialist outlook which seeks mechanical and simplistic explanations, the spiritual is happy with mystery; it does not want to understand everything because it knows that there is far too much going on in our world for any person to understand it all. On the other hand, the spiritual person has a clear vision of where he or she believes things are going and as a result is purposeful. His or her values are clearly expressed, people-focused and inclusive. As a result he or she is valued by others in the group. The spiritual person is confident, has a strong sense of fulfilment and shows a depth of character and commitment to truth and honesty which attracts others. He or she is regarded by others as a person of integrity.

All of this may sound to you like naïve, wishful thinking. You may be saying to yourself "I have never met anyone like this". But you have probably never met anyone like the person with a materialist outlook described in the previous section.

Remember that these are pictures of the extremes of a spectrum and many would agree that in the west we used to be closer to the spiritual end of the spectrum and are now being pushed towards the materialist end.

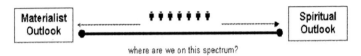

where are we on this spectrum?

Somewhere in the middle?

Of course, in reality people's understanding of life falls somewhere along the spectrum of the two extremes which have been described. Most people in the west are caught up in materialist pressures, because on average they have more disposable income than ever before, but not usually to such an extent that they are incapable of responding to the needs of others. Most people are drawn in both directions and conscientiously try to find the right path for themselves and those close to them. If we develop more fully our spiritual view of life we will find more reward and more fulfilment than if we allow ourselves to be dominated by a more material outlook.

If you are with me so far, you will have an idea of what a spiritual understanding of life is about. The spirit impinges on our existence whether we choose it or not. Some of us find ourselves explicitly searching for it because we have had an experience which has stimulated the search; others of us are oblivious of its existence until something amazing or terrifying or earth-shaking happens to us and causes us to think hard about our way of life; yet others feel that they have found it in the way that they have been brought up – perhaps in a church or faith group or in a creative family or among a set of friends – and are not interested in looking elsewhere; and many feel that there is no such thing as the spiritual life and that all is finite, limited and explained in material terms. Wherever we stand along this spectrum the spirit is not only looking for us but has implanted a spark in our very humanness which one day will make us aware of that eternal essence of life.

Some points to consider

1. Does the materialist-spiritual spectrum make sense for you? Is it a helpful pointer to what is happening in our modern age?
2. Do the arguments about the role of the media ring true for you? Can you think of examples of programmes, films or publications which pander to the materialist viewpoint? Can you think of others that have a stronger spiritual content?
3. Can you identify with the spiritual outlook and start to characterise the things which a spiritual person might hold dear?

2. We are all spiritual

The first spark

Have you ever felt inspired by nature? A breathtaking sunset over the ocean or a river. The view from a mountain peak over the surrounding terrain. The exquisite colours and shapes of flowers in a garden. The astonishing development and growth of animal life. The range of colours in a woodland walk. The beauty of fish swimming in clear sunlit water. The amazing purity and touch of a snowflake. The smell of the air after a short burst of rain. The sound of birds singing in the garden. The taste of newly picked strawberries.

Have you ever been drawn out of yourself by human achievement? The beauty of a painting. The uplifting harmonies of a piece of music. The challenge of a well-structured novel. The design of an artefact like a motor car or a piece of furniture. The explanation of scientific structures. The glories of choral singing. The pleasure of a well-constructed garden or woodland. The taste of home-made ice-cream. The ideas given birth by viewing a lovely sculpture. The teamwork of a move in a game of football leading to a wonderful goal.

Have you ever been moved to tears by evidence of human caring? The love of a spouse or partner. Selfless caring for an elderly relative. Hour-by-hour comforting of a dying friend. The giving of all to the nurture of a child with a terminal disease. The courage of someone fighting through flames to save another's life. People taking in a stranger when their home is damaged. The commitment of partners in a marriage ceremony. The joy on a child's face on achieving success or praise. The innocence of the very young. The willingness to walk many extra miles for a friend. Someone taking a drop in wages rather than see a friend lose their job. People giving up their savings to support a family on the other side of the world which has lost everything as a result of natural disaster. The spirit of resistance to injustice, even in the face of unbearable suffering. Continuing against all the odds to fight for justice and freedom. The desire to get to the truth.

Have you ever had an overwhelming feeling that life is good? Have you ever felt that life is worth living, simply because it is? Have you ever been amazed by the wonder of creation and the interconnectedness of all living things? Have you ever sat back in awe at the wonders all around you when you take time to notice?

Such feelings about the sacredness of what we call life are shared by human beings everywhere; they form the foundation for a spiritual understanding of life for those who love life.

Have you ever felt that you have a guardian angel? Many people now and in the past have had a strong sense of being watched over benignly by someone, usually thought of in spirit form though sometimes recognisable in human form, mainly invisible though continuously present. Some ancient people believed that all human beings have a star looking after them in the heavens and to this star they return when they die. Others had the concept of a daimon (or daemon), usually taking an animal form, which was the outward image of their soul, and which kept an eye on them in key moments of decision or danger. These are variants on the idea of a guardian angel, who fulfils various roles for the human being: watching over and protecting you; providing guidance, rather like a mentor, and helping you to think through problems; acting as an ally and friend, believing in you and encouraging you in your moments of difficulty; and keeping you in touch with the real you, your essence, in an attempt to keep you true to yourself. In other words, the guardian angel keeps you spiritually alert. Not only is this a lovely and comforting idea, but most people will attest to its truth in some form. How many times have you had the experience of being warned or reassured or given clarity from a source which you cannot clearly identify but which seems to come from within? Perhaps your guardian angel is your soul in action.

Have you ever had a strong sense of fate in your life? This is fate in the sense of an occasional intervention, irregular and unexpected, which causes you to act differently or feel forced to carry out a particular action. Usually we attribute our actions to fate retrospectively but such incidents influence our behaviour and decision-making. We feel that there is a spiritual force pointing us in a particular direction. The experience is not dissimilar to the guardian angel's intervention. (Note that fate is not the same as fatalism which is a conviction that all that happens in life are outside one's control.)

Have you ever felt strongly that you are unique, that there is no one else like you? Our experience of life tells us that this is the case. We are encouraged by science to believe that there are only two sets of factors which determine our development as human beings – heredity and environment. But we have only to look at the uniqueness of individuals to question this idea. In addition much of the research into identical twins confirms that, whilst there are some areas where common genes and shared nurture lead to very similar outcomes, there are many others where this does not seem to be the case; in particular twins have been found to differ in the way they think and show creativity. This supports the argument that every human being is unique.

Theories about heredity and environment seem to ignore the feeling that all of us have that we are unique. Recent research into DNA, however, confirms that everyone is different.

Spirit

The experiences described in the previous section are shared by all human beings and have been from the earliest days of human life on this planet. Such experiences are signs of the spirit at work in us and around us – the spirit which lifts us out of ourselves towards what is best (that which is full of beauty, truth and goodness) in human life. This spirit encourages us to seek the best, even in the most difficult and depressing of circumstances. Human beings are not born as mindless automata, programmed to act in particular ways, incapable of choosing or of achieving wonderful things. We are given different potential in terms of physical, intellectual and emotional make-up, but the common feature of humanity is that we are born with a soul (which will be explained in the next chapter) which enables us to respond to the spiritual, which makes us what we are, which preserves our integrity and which leads us to see that we belong both to one another and to the greater good which is humanity.

So let us explore what is meant by 'spirit' and 'spiritual'. One of the difficulties in considering the spiritual understanding of life is that both these terms are used imprecisely and this causes confusion. What follows here are definitions of the words as they are used in this book.

'Spirit' is a non-measurable energy which reveals itself in recognisable but non-material ways as a sign of inner liveliness or life-force. Spirit can be seen in all living things, including human beings; it is also seen in those objects created by living beings which evoke an active response. Thus we can speak of a person in terms of their spirit ("she has a courageous spirit" or "he made a spirited defence of the idea") or of a thing such as a painting revealing a spirit of compassion.

Sometimes spirit is used as a collective noun to refer to <u>the</u> life-force which both includes and transcends all individual spirits – the spirit. Sometimes this overarching spirit is referred to as the spirit of God or goodness.

Spiritual

This word is an adjective which is mainly used to describe people or things which reveal spirit (e.g. a spiritual place, a spiritual experience or a spiritual film). Sometimes people describe themselves as spiritual not to suggest that they reveal the spirit but because they feel sensitive to the revelation of spirit.

Often the word 'spiritual' refers more narrowly to the ultimate purpose of human existence; and, for those who put their trust in <u>the</u> spirit, 'spiritual' means that which is of God e.g. the attributes of God (goodness, love, beauty, truth, peace, forgiveness, friendship, trust, courage, sacrifice, giving). This has led to 'spiritual' being associated with eternal, ultimate perfection and with the idea that the spirit is actively seeking to transform us for our own benefit.

There is a tendency in this day and age to explain everything in scientific and material terms. Human beings have bodies made up of bone, blood, sinew, nerves, electrical signals, and so on; these components can increasingly be defined, measured, simulated and designed, so much so that science is on the way to being able to create and manipulate a human body. We also have brains, which control our body, and minds which are capable of learning and conceptualising; our brains have developed (and continue to develop) and differentiate us from other animals. We have also been given the ability to feel emotion towards other elements of the world in which we live, including other people, and the human sciences have shown us how these emotions can be manipulated by adopting certain strategies. This scientific and materialist paradigm would have us believe that we know almost everything that there is to know about being human and are capable of replicating and controlling humanity.

However, you do not need to be a scientist to realise that each human being is more than just the sum of his or her parts. We see all around us examples of strength of character that enables people to refuse to be manipulated, of genius that can create something completely new and unforeseen, of willingness to ignore conventional ideas of self-seeking in making sacrifices for others, and of such desire for freedom that no-one, however strong, violent or corrupt, can extinguish it. These are for me signs of people being filled with the spirit which exists to set us free from the forces of evil and darkness in the world.

Spiritual people have an unchanging commitment to kindness, generosity and love; they are angered by poverty and unfairness; they are committed in practical ways to building communities and making justice real; they see their own well-being as closely tied to the well-being of unnamed strangers in other parts of the world. And they do these things because they have a strong sense of wonder at and reverence for life, they see miracles everywhere and take joy in the mysteries of life and they place trust in people and in the ultimate value of every life.

Being spiritual, then, is living your life in such a way as to enable the spirit to flourish. It was suggested earlier that the spirit is the life-force through which we can see what is best in human life and seek it out. Being sensitive to the spirit causes you to live your life in such a way that you always seek what is best for yourself, for others and for the world as a whole. Sometimes there is a conflict between these, and the soul has the job of finding the best way forward in situations of conflict. How it does this will be explained in later chapters.

Spirituality

'Spirituality' is a word that has only come into common English parlance in the last 50 years, though it has been common elsewhere in the world for much longer. It is used in many different contexts, so much so that some people feel that it is so vague as to be meaningless; it needs explanation. Spirituality refers to the way in which spirit is revealed. So Buddhist spirituality is the way in which Buddhism reveals the things of the spirit; new age spirituality is the way in which new age belief systems reveal the spirit; and John Lennon's spirituality is the way he revealed the spiritual side of his life. Often spirituality refers to a specific path or practice.

For me it is how one is spiritual i.e. the way in which our soul performs its jobs in making us unique individuals. Everyone has a spirituality; it does not for the most part take a religious form, though for some people it does. Our spirituality is particular to each of us. It is the way in which our soul channels our desires, our genius and our energy in a balanced response to spiritual matters.

The rest of this book is about how spiritual people live, but let us consider two key ingredients to illustrate spirituality. The first is gratitude. It is not possible to be spiritual without a fundamental sense of thankfulness at being alive. Even in the tough times, that sense must be present. A person who is filled with bitterness or regret, who has a chip on their shoulder, or who is always looking back at what might have been has to learn to release him or herself from these burdens in order to be truly spiritual. A sense of delight at the world and its beauty in all areas is essential. This is what gives us a sense of ease with life and enables us to enjoy it. Being able to laugh, to enjoy a good meal, to delight at the beauty of nature are all essential components of the truly spiritual life.

The second is peace and freedom from anxiety. Many people live their lives anxiously and fearfully, wondering what lies around the corner. Spiritual people, who focus on allowing the soul to do its job, are far less fretful and worried because their lives are characterised by trust – in life, in the world and in others. If you believe that all will be well, then you receive a calmness and joy which has an eternal quality; it is not an occasional experience in the middle of a life of stress, it is an underpinning approach to life which enables one to put anxious, fearful and stressful moments in perspective. Our modern world has become anxious about everything and looks for ways of solving all problems; perhaps this is a reflection of the scientific, technological and information age in which we want to know everything. We need to step back and recognise three truths:

1. no individual can know everything;
2. even if we had (access to) all the facts, interpreting them is by no means straightforward;
3. many things in life are simply mysterious and incapable of explanation.

If we accept this, then there is no point in getting worked up. Rather we should seek to cultivate our soul through which we are given wisdom to be able to handle all of the issues that confront us in life. We often talk about receiving insights; they come to us from beyond our consciousness and we cannot explain where they come from. Obviously they are influenced by knowledge and experience which we have acquired, but insights are evidence that the soul is at work giving us wisdom. As we will discover in the next chapter, the soul is fed by the spirit and manifests itself in giving us good ideas, a fertile imagination, interesting stories, uplifting poems, exciting images, inspiring dreams, joyful interaction with other people; it reflects on all the things happening to us day-by-day, mulls over them, and uses them to reinforce our individual approach to life. If we trust, as the soul urges us to do, anxiety significantly reduces. It will never totally disappear, because we need some anxiety to avoid walking into dangerous situations, but it will cease to dominate our lives and allow a peaceful frame of mind to enter and stay.

What is meant by the word God?

The previous sections have used the term God and so it also needs to be defined. Many people today have unhelpful ideas of who or what God is. They think in terms of a person (an old man with a grey or white beard sitting on a throne in a place called heaven) or a judge (a fierce warrior, wielding thunderbolt in the sky, who will vanquish those who do not obey him) or a rule-maker (an ageless man who wrote on tablets of stone the rules for living). Notice that these ideas are reflections of a society in which men ruled in a hierarchical fashion and pictured God in their own image. Such ideas are anachronistic.

God is the word used to refer to the energy which is at the heart of all spiritual experience and is seeking to lift us out of our inward-looking human selves; God is within us and around us in the world. There are all sorts of words used to say this (e.g. transcendent power, ultimate horizon, depth of being, everlasting life) but they all amount to the same thing – the spirit of God is that which enables us to rise above ourselves. God is the most commonly used word for 'ultimate reality', 'the ground of being', 'being itself', 'isness'. As Moses reported in the Old Testament, he met God who said 'I am who I am'. God is the mystery at the root of our universe, beyond all naming.

In most religions, God is spoken of in personal terms, because that seems to be the natural way to speak of the spirit with whom our relationship is personal, who seems to many to have a person-like presence in their lives, and who speaks to them in various ways through what happens in their lives. One may not be able to conceive of God as a person-like being but at the same time not have a problem with people using personal descriptors if they reflect their experience. For example, it is hardly surprising that Christians speak of God in personal terms since they believe that God is revealed most fully in the person of Jesus Christ who himself spoke to, and of, God in personal terms.

People have two main concepts of God: one sees God as supernatural and external; the other sees God as all-encompassing and internal. The supernatural view imagines God as person-like, up in heaven, beyond the universe, separate from the world despite having created it. This God occasionally intervenes in human affairs, usually spectacularly, and can be asked through prayer to intervene.

The all-encompassing view imagines God as the spirit in whom every living thing lives. God is the one in whom 'we live and move and have our being' as Paul says in the Acts of the Apostles in the Christian New Testament. Where are we in relation to God? We are in God; God is not out-there but right-here, all around us. God is present in all things, aware of all things and transcends all things; this God does not intervene but is continuously present; prayer is not about calling for God's intervention but seeking to align our wills with God.

God is ultimate goodness, truth, love, beauty, peace, justice and excellence; you may think of other terms. These ideals exist whether we acknowledge them or not and whether we agree on their nature or not. They are exemplified in our world and exist in many forms. We may disagree about what goodness is but we usually agree that there is a perfection to which we can all aspire which is independent of individual standards. We share common notions of it when we examine practical examples; we measure them against our own notion of perfection and in so doing we acknowledge that there is such an ideal.

Our soul within us reaches out to the spirit around us and, if we allow the spiritual dimension of our lives to flourish, we are impelled towards ultimate goodness. Of course, our sensitivity towards the spiritual side of our nature varies. Some people have less inclination towards goodness than others and will continue in what we might call self-centredness, but this does not mean that their spiritual side is entirely missing. We often meet people who in some areas of life seem cruel and unjust but who in particular circumstances are drawn towards the good. The fact is that just as any human faculty (e.g. physical skill, mental agility) can be enhanced and toned by exercise, training and concentration, so our spiritual dimension can be strengthened. If people spend all their time in sordid conditions or see few glimpses of love or are surrounded by violence or never experience peace, it is not surprising that their spiritual faculty is eroded. If, on the other hand, they experience love, trust, freedom, encouragement and growth, then they are more likely to develop their spiritual faculty. Just as we need to breathe physical air to grow physically, so we need to breathe spiritual air to grow spiritually. Human growth requires both.

We are starting to get something of an idea about the character of what we call God. The spirit of God is the spirit of those things which contribute to goodness (or whatever we want to call the ideal). God is always positive and constructive, never negative and destructive. God is the love which cares for people, builds them up and leads them to freedom, i.e. not simply the absence of hatred. God is the peace which brings calm, assurance and protection, i.e. not simply the absence of strife. God is the beauty which shows us how things can be perfect, inspiring and challenging, i.e. not simply the absence of filth and crudity. God is the justice which ensures that the underdog and outcast is cared for and enriched, i.e. not simply the application of rules of law. God is the mercy which offers forgiveness to those who recognise that they have let themselves and others down and want to change, i.e. emphatically not a god of revenge. God is the truth which looks for honesty and right behaviour, i.e. not simply the absence of falseness. God surrounds us in our day-to-day life in a specific setting with all that is best about life and people.

This vision of God is of perfection, of what humans could be if they allowed their lives to be governed by the spiritual side of their nature. They would find spiritual enrichment by knowing that they are in the presence of the spirit of God and they would seek to live out a full life on earth knowing that they were engaged in those behaviours which are everlasting, loyal to the inheritance that they have received from our ancestors and loyal to the future which is to be passed on to those who come after us.

Idea of 'thin places'

We began this chapter by thinking about some experiences that we have all from time to time enjoyed. They were described as signs of the spiritual dimension of our lives, those occasions when we are lifted out of the ordinary and everyday into a realm that has an eternal feel to it. The idea of 'thin places' comes from Celtic spirituality and refers to those places and times when we have a strong experience of being grounded, when the spiritual and the material realms of our existence come together and we are able to sense something of the spiritual whilst located in the material. The Celts sought such places and considered them holy.

Such a place might be at the site of an ancient tree which spoke to them of the reliability and constancy of nature; I had a similar moment of vision in front of a kauri tree in New Zealand. It might be on the coast where both the power of the sea and the stillness of the sunset are experienced; there are many such locations in our country which can just amaze us with their beauty. It might be at a sacred spot where a holy person was murdered for her beliefs and we feel almost tangibly the presence of faith and goodness. It might be in a church or a castle where we have an acute awareness of the presence of those who have gone before and can feel their commitment to those who would follow them. It might be in a graveyard where the resting places of those who have given their lives for a particular cause evoke a strong sense of their courage and loyalty.

These thin places are where we are drawn out of our preoccupation with today's problems and concerns to consider other (usually higher) values, other (usually eternal) timescales and other (usually inspiring) causes. This is the spiritual side of our humanity being called into action and sadly today for many of us we do not find thin places often enough. The next chapters will help us to find them more often.

Some points to consider

1. Can you identify some experiences that have made you intensely aware of the sacredness of life?
2. Do the distinctions between spirit, spiritual and spirituality make sense for you?
3. Can you see why gratitude and freedom from anxiety might be two key dimensions of a spiritual person?

4. Does the explanation of the term God help or hinder you? In what ways?
5. Do you find the idea of thin places helpful? Can you think of any such places in your life?

3. Soul matters

The idea of soul

Some early ideas about human beings suggested that each person had four dimensions - physical (represented by the body), intellectual (the mind), emotional (the heart) and spiritual (the soul). Although these were differentiated in order to discuss their functions and effects, it was recognised that each human being had all four dimensions, that they were integrated and that none of them could work independently from the others. Thus it would be emphasised that the body cannot operate without the mind determining its actions, the mind is influenced by the heart at all times, the body is often the source of feelings, and the soul is what integrates the other three in a unique way in each individual. The soul was seen as that element within the human being that both provides a window through which the spirit illuminates the individual's thinking, decision-making and actions and generates his/her spirituality. This perhaps can be understood in diagrammatic form (on the next page).

The soul became seen as the location of religious belief, and gradually it became so closely associated with religious belief that it was conceived as entirely separate from the other components of human-ness and capable of eternal life.

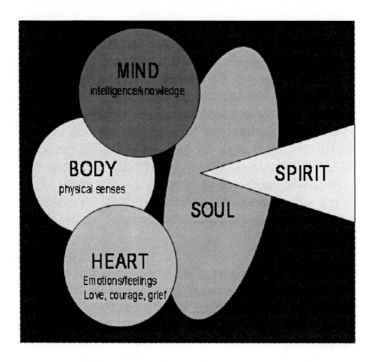

This led to all sorts of confusing and difficult ideas (e.g. souls in torment, purgatory, immortality, indulgences) that need to be left in the past. This is unfortunate because in suggesting the idea of the soul the early thinkers were simply giving a name to human faculty which deals with the spiritual understanding of life. As often happens, words change their meanings and it is difficult to continue to use them without causing confusion. In reasserting the soul as essential to human life a definition of the word is needed, especially since, as a result of the decline in religious belief in the western world, the word is no longer in common usage.

This book uses the word 'soul' to mean the faculty which enables human beings to appreciate and reach out to the spiritual dimension of their existence. All human beings have such a faculty. It cannot be identified or measured scientifically as it is not an organ like the brain or the heart, but the existence of a faculty called here the soul is verified by the fact that people to varying degrees have experience of the spiritual, as described in the previous chapter. The modern age's lack of understanding of 'soul' is very different from the previous thousands of years of human existence when the soul was well understood and frequently discussed. Perhaps we will become more familiar with talking about our souls as we become more aware (along with many scientists) that not all things are capable of scientific analysis and explanation. Some things are simply mysterious.

Our soul is not just part of a human being, it is what we are, the essence of our being. It is our identity, what makes us who we are, and in that sense it has three jobs to do for us – one is to energise us, the second is to receive and process spiritual signals and the third is to build our identity, our uniqueness and our integrity, thereby expressing our spirituality.

1. The first job is to give life to human beings beyond the physical. We are all born physically from our mother's womb, we inherit a genetic make-up, we learn through our senses and we grow as life-forms. However, our experience of living, right from birth, goes far beyond what our physical senses and mental processing capability give to us. We speak of the innocence of children, their imagination and their awareness of important things. This is what makes them unique and individual, it is what moulds their personality, it is what gives them the desire to grow and learn and conquer and develop. Part of it is the natural instinct for survival but much more of it draws on the

ability to see that there is more to human life than the everyday. This is the life-force which empowers and drives every human being; it is not about surviving, it is about enjoying the wonders of life and using the imagination.

We know all about this first job from the way in which we use the word soul in talking about *soul* music or to describe someone who is the life and *soul* of a party or a group; in both cases we are referring to something or someone with energy, life, vibrancy and purpose. These words give us an idea of what the soul is – it is what drives us, it is what makes us realise that life is wonderful and worth living, it is what makes us feel delight in all the beautiful things, places and people around us. It is what fills us with excitement and joie de vivre, it is what inspires our desire to achieve and to enjoy and it is what gives us energy to keep moving forward.

2. The second job is linked closely to the first; the soul enables us to see beyond the physical world which surrounds us into the immaterial, spiritual world which gives purpose and delight to life. Our eyes see, our tongues taste, our hands feel, our noses smell, our ears hear – they take in the physical stimuli – but our souls give us insight, intuition, premonition and experience of eternity. Our souls enable us to identify and seek the best things in life, those things which are most fulfilling. Our soul is less concerned with minimising discomfort and more concerned with inspiring us to achieve and experience things which are beyond day-to-day existence.

You would think from current political priorities and media interests that people are only interested in the material world, but nothing could be further from the truth. People are increasingly reacting against the short-term and selfish society which has developed in recent years and are searching for the spiritual – peace, beauty, fulfilment, courage, grace and meaning – which human beings since our origins have valued. Our body can react to sense stimuli, our brain can generate appropriate physical and mental responses but it is our soul that makes us aware of the non-material, non-physical aspects of life. It sees the beauty of a painting, it recognises the graceful action, it applauds the courageous sacrifice, it looks for meaning and purpose; in other words the soul is our vehicle for experiencing the spiritual and eternal dimension of life.

This job is illustrated in the diagram below. At the centre of all existence is the spirit of goodness described in the previous chapter and sometimes called God. It is all around us. Around the spirit in the simple model in the diagram are individual souls, located in you, me and all human beings. These souls are our means of receiving the spirit; we experience the spirit through our souls, each of us receiving our own signals. Our own spirit is formed by our soul reflecting on the spirit signals together with all the other things going on in our lives.

3. The third job of the soul is to make sense of things which are going on around us and happening to us. By doing so it provides balance and integrity in our lives. It reflects on what is going on, it collates the spirit signals, it uses our time of sleep to wrestle with challenges and confusion, and it reconciles conflict whilst operating in the background. Clearly the mind is involved in all this processing but the soul has the responsibility of sorting out meaning, purpose and relationships in life.

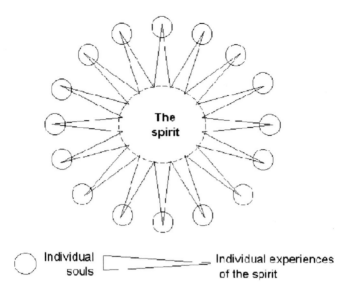

○ Individual souls ◁─────── Individual experiences of the spirit

It does this by helping us to formulate a world-view of our own. A world-view is an interpretation of what is going on in the mystery of life so that we are able not only to remain sane and focused but so that when challenges come to us we are able to make sense of them and put them in context. When we speak about the integrity of a person, this is what we mean; a person with integrity has been able to develop a world-view to which they are committed. All that they say and do is consistent. If we look after our soul, we acquire an eternal view of human life which is thrilling and inspiring for us and for all those around us.

The soul holds us together, keeps us whole, integrates all the conflicting pressures that we experience and gives us our uniqueness. The soul helps us to find balance so that we do not disintegrate and fall apart. The first job is about energy, drive, excitement and delight; the third is about not letting any of these get out of hand at the expense of destroying our essential person.

It should be noted that some people use the word 'spirit' instead of 'soul' to mean the same thing, but this book differentiates the soul from the spirit. It sees the soul as a human faculty which reflects on both the spiritual and the everyday events of our lives in developing our own spirit (i.e. who we are in a rounded and holistic sense). Our souls digest our spiritual experiences (which may be of other people's spirits as well as from the natural and animal world) to develop a rounded spirit in ourselves which is then experienced by other people. This is illustrated below.

In the middle ages, people wrote at length about the soul in all living things – a source of powerful energy which is nonetheless under control.

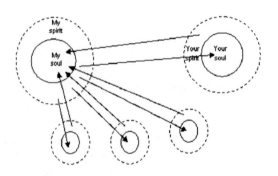

However, because we are treating the soul as a human faculty, the energy in plants and animals should preferably be called their spirit. We see it when, for example, we see plants and trees thrusting forward, almost despite the barriers that are put in their way, almost knowing when and where to do so; or when we see animals with the same sort of inquisitive and excitable behaviour as humans but also knowing when to curb their enthusiasm if it is dangerous or unwise. This idea of the omnipresence of soul (or spirit) in the natural world is one that we have lost, largely because in an industrial and post-industrial world people no longer have direct contact with the natural world. This is regrettable because we have also lost sight of the interconnectedness of all living things; we have become willing to damage the world in which we live in part because we no longer have a sense of sharing so much in common with plant and animal life.

The soul's big picture

I have referred to having a world-view a few times, so perhaps we should think about what that means. Our world-view is our image of reality, how we see and interpret what has happened, what is happening and what might happen to us in the future; some would call it our "big picture". Everyone has a world-view; we acquire it through the process of growing up. We use it to explain what is going on around us and it shapes our decisions. Our reaction to an extraordinary news item (i.e. do we think that it is credible?) is governed by our world-view.

There are as many world-views as there are people but they tend to have similarities. We are moulded by culture (family, society, language, school, workplace and other settings in which we spend time) and this causes similarities of world-view. For the purposes of this book two world-views have been highlighted: the spiritual and the materialist. The spiritual world-view sees beyond the physical world of our daily experience to a non-material level of reality, which we call spirit. The material world-view sees nothing beyond the physical world of time and energy governed by natural laws; it has no place for an inexplicable energy called spirit. It is sometimes called the scientific world-view because it has reduced everything to basic elements that can be measured, with no room for faith or courage or love or mystery;

everything is seen as mechanistic and reductionist. But not all scientists take this view; increasingly science makes use of words like 'relative', 'uncertain', 'mysterious', 'fuzzy' in reflecting the interconnectedness of life which demands an holistic and organic viewpoint and a more humble and reverent approach to life on earth.

Our world-view affects the way we live our lives, makes us who we are, determines our values and shapes our personalities. The spiritual world-view is beyond time (sometimes called transcendent) and enables us to be aware of truths which are not immediately obvious. A spiritual understanding of life promotes deep and authentic, rather than superficial, living, enabling us to become human beings in the fullest sense. Through it we become more aware of purpose and meaning in life as we seek ultimate truth. If people do not have such an understanding, their lives lack meaning, grounding and identity; in summary their lives lack depth.

The spiritual world-view arises from our human-ness and so is inclusive of all people. It is not narrow or dogmatic; it is exploratory and experiential, recognising the worth of others' discoveries; it is always provisional and dynamic, developing as we learn more about the world; it is open rather than closed. It is not just concerned with our inner lives but with all aspects of life and living. The individual's experience of spirituality is never in isolation from others'. It emphasises the sacred in people and places and encourages a sense of reverence and compassion for all of creation.

For a full and deep life all people need to be benefiting from a spiritual world-view and our soul gives it to us. Our mind can assimilate facts, ideas and structures, our emotions and experience help us to relate to people, our culture and education leads us towards particular lines of conclusion, but it is our soul which takes these raw materials for each one of us and converts them into a consistent world-view that reflects our uniqueness as individuals and protects our integrity. This does not happen overnight; it needs long periods of reflection and contemplation; it involves patience and being slow to judge; it requires time pondering the subtlety and nuances of our living. The soul is busy doing these things all the time but it needs help from us. We have to feed it with times of quiet and wonder, times of pleasure and joy, times of mystery and uncertainty as well as the things of everyday life. Ultimately the work of the soul is to encourage us to place our trust in the world and its people, through intuition, generosity and encouragement. The soul enjoys complexity and subtlety, wonder and elegance, incompleteness and ambiguity because it can try out these dimensions against its world-view.

All people have a world-view of some sort, but for many it is shallow and superficial, capable of change at the slightest impulse. It lacks depth. The soul gives depth. Some people only start to think about depth when a tragic event overtakes them and forces them to think hard about their world-view. At this point, their soul is prompting them to reflect and to consider their need for a deeper, more grounded, more eternal world-view.

Soulful, spiritual people

So what do soulful, spiritual people look like, how would you recognise one?

First of all, they would be very conscious that they live in a world that does not belong to them or to others who currently share it with them. This world needs to be cared for because it has been given in trust for a short period and needs to be handed on in a better state than it was when they received it. They believe that they have inherited it from their ancestors and have it on trust for their successors. They see the world as a sacred place and everything in it (atmosphere, minerals, land, sea, plants, animals and other humans) must be cared for in order to foster growth and development. They have a strong sense of continuity and this stretches back to the beginning of time on earth and stretches forward to the end of time. They are conscious of living for a short period in a world that has existed and will exist infinitely longer than they can imagine.

Secondly, they would exude a sense of gratitude and joy. Soulful people are grateful for life, for people, for places, for artefacts, for ideas, for the past, for the present and for the future because they are conscious of living in a wonderful world which is dynamically changing as it showers gifts on us while we are alive in this place. They have a strong sense of wonder, similar to that given to a growing child, and pursue knowledge for its own sake and as a force for liberation. The soulful person sees the world and its inhabitants as basically good, despite the inhuman things that are happening everyday. No-one can comprehend everything about life, but the spiritual person will seek to know more and to celebrate the wonders of the universe and the life-enhancing achievements of humans.

Thirdly, they would come across as calm, peaceful and reflective. Because they have a strong sense of the ultimate goodness of the world and its people, anxiety and fear are less of a problem than they are for others. Instead of rushing around in a mad panic as seems to have become the norm, the soulful person takes time out to think, to learn and to reflect on what is going on in his or her life. This makes him or her more attentive to the needs of others, to the good things that are happening as well as the bad, and to what needs to be done to address some of these concerns. Because they take a longer perspective on life, are able to see things in context and are confident about ultimate value, soulful people are not rattled by the short-term and immediate. They have a strong sense of purpose and meaning in life. This does not make them impervious to the ups and downs of life or unconcerned about the many unpleasant things that human beings are capable of, but it does allow them to react in a calmer and more reflective way as the spirit requires. But they are not just thinkers, they are also doers.

Fourthly, they would care greatly for all, and especially those in need of any kind. Because soulful people have a strong sense of community and humanity (other people anywhere in the world are their brothers and sisters and matter), they seek every opportunity for people to grow and develop and experience true freedom. Thus they will fight for justice and equality of opportunity for all people. This will bring them into conflict with those who are protecting their own interests at the expense of others. No-one should believe that the spiritual life is without pain and struggle, but the pain and the struggle can be handled with greater courage, firmness and patience by those whose lives are not dominated by the short-term. Soulful people pursue freedom (by removing the chains of poverty, ignorance and violence) for all people, for whom they care with an everlasting love.

Fifthly, soulful people are open and generous to others. Because a fundamental principle for them is that all people are born equal and are deserving of every opportunity to grow and develop, they are open to other people's needs and desires. They try to make sure that nothing stands in other people's way and always set out to build them up. They try to be generous with their time and resources in dealing with others, believing that all that they have is a gift which they have been given to share with others. They will, of course, come across situations and people which horrify them, but, conscious of their own weaknesses and failings, they try to avoid being judgemental. They have a strong sense of the grace and mercy which has surrounded their life and seek to be a friend to all. They have a vision of how life should be in a perfect state and they set out to create this for all with whom they have contact. When they see people in trouble or situations of unimaginable cruelty and hatred, they look for a healing way forward rather than a judgemental solution.

Finally, soulful people have a strong sense of a transforming spirit at work in people and places. They believe in development towards an ultimate goal of human perfection, which may or may not be achieved, but which is of absolute importance because it inspires human beings to strive for improvement in all areas of life, especially the spiritual. The soulful person is not a naïve optimist but a grounded person who is convinced about the direction of human development and who believes that, even in times like the current one when the future for the earth and its inhabitants looks bleak, the direction is clear and the goal is unquestionably worthwhile.

The soul and trust

Our souls urge us to trust ourselves, to believe in ourselves. Too often in our modern age we are led to believe that we are not good enough for a particular activity, whether it be an everyday task, an artistic challenge or building a relationship. Our soul tells us that we are uniquely able to achieve more than we think provided that we give an activity the focus, energy, time and patience that it deserves. There is no need to think that we are not good enough so long as we are doing our best; our soul tells us to believe in ourselves and to act out of this belief especially when it comes to dealing with others.

Nelson Mandela is often quoted[1] as saying: "Our deepest fear is not that we are inadequate, our deepest fear is that

1. But actually a quote from a book by Marianne Williamson, "A Return to Love", HarperCollins, New York, 1992, pp. 190-191

we are powerful beyond measure. It is our light not our darkness that most frightens us. We ask ourselves who am I to be brilliant, gorgeous, talented and fabulous. Actually who are you not to be – you are a child of God. As we let our light shine, we unconsciously give other people permission to do the same. As we are liberated from our own fear, our presence automatically liberates others."

Our souls urge us to trust in other people. We live in an age which is full of cynicism about people. Too often we fail to see the good in people, looking only for their faults. It reminds me of a black spot on a piece of white paper; if you ask people what they can see, they almost always answer "a black spot on a white background" rather than "a sheet of white paper with a black spot on it"; they see the flaw rather than the overwhelming goodness. The soul teaches us to start from the viewpoint that people are innately good and are to be trusted; we should never play down other people's goodness but rather seek to build it up just as we would want others to believe in us and to help us on our journey. Of course, all human beings are a mix of good and bad, being pulled in both directions. This is part of our human nature, but our soul teaches us that our starting point in dealing with people should never be to assume that they are nearer to the bad end of the spectrum but nearer to the good end. We should start with an assumption that favours people rather than the reverse.

Our souls urge us to put our trust in people rather than in things. Trust is an essential component of human life but sadly the emphasis on consumerism reduces the propensity to trust people. We need to revive it. Have you noticed that you always spend less money if for some reason you cannot get out? Shops rely on our habit of browsing and purchasing what we do not really need. Our television screens are continually trying to persuade us that we should buy things that we cannot possibly live without. The social pressure on young people to wear or use or play with brand-name goods is very strong. Such consumerism is symptomatic of human beings' trust in things, of believing that things bring us happiness/fulfilment. We need to think hard about this and realise that lasting pleasure does not come from things; it comes from people.

Our souls help us to think about our priorities. We all read stories about real poverty. You may have seen a well-known image of a woman in Brazil who had lost her home, land and children, yet her arms were open in welcome to share what little she had. We face choices everyday about how we choose to live. We have to choose where we are going to place our trust. Do we trust in the idols whom the media glorify? Do we trust in the much vaunted products in our shops? Or do we trust in the spirit and in people who are driven by the spirit? Our soul has learnt what is important and we should follow its promptings to live in a simpler more caring way.

The soul and wisdom

Wisdom is a desirable attribute. We all seek out wise people when we have a problem. They are good to consult when you want to talk things over but you do not want to be told exactly what to do. They really listen to you – to how you are feeling inside as well as what you are saying. Wise people think carefully before they speak and are happy to learn from their mistakes.

The soul teaches us wisdom. Wisdom is not the same as knowledge. You have knowledge if you have the facts, the information, the theory; you have wisdom if you can apply knowledge sensibly as a result of experience and good judgement. You can be wise even if you do not get top marks for spelling. You can be wise as grown-ups or as children (e.g. the story of the emperor's new clothes). You can be wise when you are acutely aware of your ignorance and are keen to learn. You need to check whether there are any areas where you consider yourself, or others consider you, as an expert or professional, since they are the areas where you will find it hardest to be wise. If you feel that we have your status to uphold, you may become unable to speak with honesty.

The soul is full of wisdom because it spends time reflecting on events and actions and seeking explanations. We now have information about everything from everywhere at our finger tips, but we are no wiser. We know more and more about medicine but we do not listen to what our bodies are saying to us; we listen to programmes about world affairs but we do not seem to have the wisdom to deal with conflicts near at hand; we want to know about people but not to know them and to share their problems because we do not know how to solve them. If we want to be wise we need to place our trust in the soul and find ways to nurture its reflective processes.

Some points to consider

1. This book makes a point of distinguishing between soul and spirit whereas others use the terms interchangeably. Does the distinction help you?
2. The soul is described as having three jobs to do for us. Do these jobs need to be done and, if so, how do you think that they are carried out if not by a faculty such as that called here the soul?
3. Does the idea of having a 'big picture' make sense for you? If so, what is your 'big picture' and how does it acquire depth?
4. At the end of the first chapter you were asked to characterise the things that a spiritual person might hold dear. Has the description of soulful, spiritual people in this chapter clarified

your earlier ideas? Can you think of other characteristics of being spiritual?

5. The final paragraphs emphasise trust and wisdom. Are they important for you? Can you see how the soul might enhance them?

4.   Feeding the soul

You will realise from what has been said so far that the soul is the key to one's spiritual life; in other words, the soul matters. We need to spend some time, therefore, thinking about how we can help our soul to grow so that it is more in tune with the life of the spirit. In this chapter we will remind ourselves what the soul is and what it does, consider what a fully functioning soul might look like and examine some of the reasons for under-performance. We will then look at ways of feeding the soul.

Demystifying the soul

The first thing to emphasise is that we should not regard the soul as lacking substance simply because it is impossible to locate it physically or measure its size. The soul is the name given to the human faculty which integrates our mind, heart and body; our minds give us the ability to think, reflect, conceptualise, investigate and communicate; we picture our heart as giving us the ability to feel, care, love, respond; and our body receives and transmits the signals from other people and things as inputs to our intellectual, emotional and physical processing. The soul sits behind these other processes trying to make sense of what is happening in our world; it brings together seemingly random feelings and experiences, reflects on them, has insights, comes up with unexpected ideas in looking for the right course of action; it works in background mode, sifting, observing, connecting; but above all it is on the lookout for spiritual activity which inspires and enthuses. By doing these things the soul gives unity and integrity to our mind, heart and body processes, and creates in us our essence or uniqueness. It does not operate in the clouds but in the concrete situations of everyday life where it gathers its source material. All the details of the ways we pass our time are under observation from within by our soul in its desire to help us to make sense of our lives and find fulfilment. We become the people we are because of the actions of the soul in patiently sifting through our experiences, weighing up our impulses, exploring the confusing and mysterious elements of our lives, analysing what makes us feel good, etc. The soul brings clarity to our lives - sometimes unexpectedly - perhaps a sense of special occasion, a sudden change of mind, an unforeseen outcome, a need to act – and sometimes slowly as part of a gradual awakening, as our soul considers events and ponders people's reactions.

Our souls are concerned with deep rather than surface living; they ask questions, try to interpret, cross-relate and search; they are not satisfied with the glib and superficial. They are interested in what adds value to living rather than in doing things for their own sake; they encourage us to look for importance and ultimate purpose rather than the immediate. They want us to enjoy lasting and meaningful relationships which help us to grow as human beings rather than short-term flings that leave us confused or dissatisfied. They look for experiences which are meaningful and consistent with our inner self. We all know when our soul is pleased with us; it is when we have an overwhelming sense of satisfaction, a feeling of being at one with the world, a desire to press onward, a pleasure at the outcome of hard work and a conviction that we are doing the right thing. Such feelings reassure and strengthen us and enable us both to know real and deep joy and to feel able to face any situation with equanimity.

A fully functioning soul

By now you may have a good idea of what a fully functioning soul is like but let me go further and identify some requirements in the individual for the soul to function well. Each requirement is accompanied by an explanation of why it is important.

A fully functioning soul requires you to:

- *have a reliable, though not necessarily large, group of family and friends who can offer a listening ear and honest advice.*
  Human beings are social animals whose purpose is to work together for the good of the world. We depend on one another and learn from one another. The soul needs the sharing of ideas, confidences, alternative views and love in order to do its job - most effectively through a small group of people who are close to you. Spiritual growth requires us to be honest about our own weaknesses, not lying or distorting the truth; spiritual health is about honesty.

- *be open to, and on the lookout for, new and enriching ideas, people, places and things, both close at hand and further afield.*
  The soul constantly wants us to take a broader view of who we are and how we should relate to others. Some people are held back by pre-conceived ideas of who they are, brought on perhaps by their childhood, physical condition, sense of inadequacy, educational difficulties or emotional confusion. The soul wants us to grow in all areas of life; this involves us in moving away from thoughts about self towards greater awareness of other people and the broader world.

- *develop an interest in other cultures, belief-systems, ideas, values and ethics.*
  The soul works within each of us to help us to find fulfilment and truth. This involves us in finding out about other ways of living (especially those with a moral dimension) so that we can evaluate and compare them in the process of refining our own world-view.

- *be prepared to work hard and make extra effort when called upon.*
  The soul is the source of our energy and drive but these can only flourish successfully in a person who is prepared to work hard, give time and wrestle with problems. There is nothing more satisfying than the feelings one gets on completion of a piece of hard work, on the solving of a difficult problem or at the successful end-point of a lengthy project.

- *have a strong sense of feeling grounded in the natural world and our history and heritage.*
  The soul takes its pleasure and inspiration from the wonders of creation and the way our ancestors responsibly developed our world. It is fed by spending time exploring the beauty of nature and learning about how life was lived in previous times.

- *be enthusiastic about art, literature and music.*
  Nothing stirs and stimulates the soul more than beauty, and human beings' self-expression through works of art plays a key role in reminding the soul of beautiful things. The soul wants to look upon aesthetically pleasing objects, to hear uplifting music, to read challenging books, to see engaging films and to

listen to worthwhile conversation. It wants to be stimulated by beauty as part of the evidence of the spirit's presence.

- *recognise the importance of solitude and quietness to allow for meaningful reflection.*
  The great eastern religions teach us that the best way of receiving the spirit is through silence, as we patiently wait for the spirit to grow in us (like a gardener has to wait for the seeds that have been planted to grow). The soul needs time to reflect and opportunity to communicate. All religions have at their core the idea that the process of coming to know God intimately involves us in emptying ourselves of those aspects of our humanity which prevent us from thinking beyond the material so that we can embrace the eternal.

- *allow time for the soul to reflect and ponder.*
  The spiritual journey is about change, involving not so much dramatic conversion as slow seepage until our inner self is fully responsive to the spirit. This requires patience and a willingness to wait – attributes which are under threat in our modern age.

- *have knowledge of the energy for love and justice in our world and attune yourself to it.*
  Spiritual living is about making a commitment to this life-force and looking for signs of its presence in the things, places, people, events which make up our lives. The soul is fed by wonder and awe, celebrates love and joy and looks for peace and harmony. The soul wants to be nourished by compassionate and just living.

The starting point for nurturing the soul is the intellectual recognition that the spirit is not somewhere else but at the heart of our being, surrounding us and within us. The soul can then work with events, actions and experiences in the ordinary world of our lives. The spirit shines through in 'thin places', where the material and the spiritual of everyday experiences intersect (e.g. in special places, in viewing the natural world, in listening to beautiful music, in seeing a beautiful painting, in hearing a wonderful poem, in being moved by a passionate film, in engaging with emotional drama, in seeing the courage of individuals, at times of suffering and grief, in solving problems at work, in the joy of a child's first attempts to ride a cycle, in the wonderful taste of a new recipe, and so on). We all have 'thin places' in our lives and we need to be more open to them. We know that the soul has been fed when we experience joy, when we feel relaxed amid the confusion of life, when we feel grateful and when our thoughts are compassionate.

An under-performing soul
Having considered what is needed to encourage our souls to function well let us briefly turn to consider the things that stop the soul from performing. As you might expect, many of them are the converse of the things on the list which we have just examined.

A soul under-performs in people who have:

- *a self-centred outlook which causes them to believe that they are at the centre of the universe.*
  The soul cannot grow when this attitude is present because it wants to move us away from being dominated by self towards being open to others.

- *an unwillingness to see that other people's ideas and belief systems may have value.*
  The soul struggles to raise its performance in people who have pre-judged all opposing or different ideas as worthless; their minds are closed and they simply defend their current position. The soul can make little progress if there is no scope for flexibility and no willingness to change.

- *a literalist, unimaginative interpretation of life.*
  The soul operates through processes of reflection, pondering and distillation; it is happy with the mysterious, the ambiguous, the new and the unforeseen. It cannot develop in the context of hard and fast, literal interpretations.

- *a reluctance to think things through or to tackle difficult ideas.*

  The soul can only work well in a human being who is prepared to apply effort to solving problems, wrestling with doubts, and overcoming difficulties. The soul will seek to encourage greater willingness to think things through but only if there is a commitment to go down this road.

- *lack of flexibility and an unwillingness to work on learning new things.*
  The soul needs people who are ready to explore and find out; closed minds limit the soul's ability to perform well. It is rooted in flexibility; it cannot make progress with minds that are closed, dogmatic and fixed.

- *lack of spiritual inputs.*
  The soul needs to receive spiritual signals from the higher side of human life – love, beauty, truth, compassion, justice, goodness – for inspiration. These are the raw material on which it feeds.

When the soul is under-performing the individual has a strong sense of emptiness, lack of purpose and meaning, disappointment with key areas of life, absence of values, little sense of achievement, and no spiritual awareness. The soul needs to be fed just as much as the body.

Removing blockages and opening the way for the spirit

The preceding discussion has highlighted some of the ways in which we can help or hinder the soul's functioning. But there may be other reasons why our soul is not being fed. For many of us our desire to be close to the spirit is at tension with our everyday cares and concerns and so we need to tackle the things going on in our lives that prevent the soul from engaging with the spiritual dimension of our existence.

One such thing can be tiredness. Many of us have heavy burdens in our daily lives (perhaps looking after a family, perhaps nursing a loved one, perhaps combating stress in the workplace, perhaps tackling a problem that is beyond us). We need to feel able to lay down our burdens. They may be physical, mental, emotional or spiritual. We may need more bodily rest; most of us need to aim for a balanced, healthy life-style; we may need to tackle our diet and take more exercise. We may need mental rest; often we are distracted by so much going on and simply need to take time out for reflection. We may also need to relax our soul, coming as a child with a sense of wonder and gratitude, not trying too hard but simply letting the spirit bless us so that we can become a blessing to others.

A second may be the need to overcome our natural instincts for short-term pleasure and gratification, if they are dominating our lives too much. If they have got out of control in a particular way, then we need to focus on how to bring them back into balance; we can usually see the causes, even if we try to ignore them, and our spiritual life demands that we tackle the causes at their source to avoid being imprisoned by the short-term. This is about facing up to ourselves as we really are, letting the bad side come to the surface. This may be very painful but increasing self-knowledge and recognising the need for forgiveness are key to a true encounter with the spirit's transforming presence. When our false self is stripped away, we can feel the goodness and love of the spirit.

A third blockage may be that our existing spiritual understanding may be too narrow and prevents us from seeing the spirit at work in people's lives. We need to find ways of detaching ourselves from pre-conceived ideas in order for our soul to function effectively. Over the centuries the spiritual leaders have emphasised the importance of solitude in broadening our view of the spiritual life. Solitude was seen by those who retreated to the desert to be a place for liberation from one's illusions because it was in solitude that individuals had unique encounters with spiritual mysteries. Thomas Merton, a Trappist monk from Gethsemani Abbey, moved to a hermitage in the woods nearby for the last three years of his life because "it is in deep solitude that I find the gentleness with which I can truly love my brothers. The more solitary I am, the more affection I have for them. It is pure affection, and filled with reverence for the solitude of others. Solitude and silence teach me to love my brothers for what they are, not for what they say."

Many people need help with the spiritual life and seek a soul friend or spiritual director, who can offer guidance and wisdom, sharing the journey and offering some support/objectivity when we cannot see the wood for the trees. The spiritual director knows the road of spiritual growth and can help the spiritual learner to find light in the darkness, strength for struggle and hope during moments of despair. The relationship can foster spiritual growth through the mystery of shared doubts and strengthened convictions.

Nourishing the soul

The argument of this book is that, for meaning, purpose and depth in life, we should feed our soul so that we can experience day-by-day the wisdom, peace, joy, freedom and love which the soul wants us to enjoy. So how do we nourish the soul?

First of all, it should be stressed that nourishing the soul is not an abstract activity. Some people seem to think that it demands a high intellect, withdrawal from life and the embrace of a sort of other-worldliness. Nothing could be further from the truth. The soul is fed by the daily situations in which we find ourselves, the mundane and the sometimes difficult. Yes, the soul looks for inspiration (the infilling of spiritual experiences) but it also needs the so-called ordinary elements of living (family, work, relationships, pain, triumph, sadness, defeat). Its job is to take both the uplifting and the mundane experiences of real life and to make sense of them for each one of us, moulding our character and refining our integrity. There is a continual dialogue going on within the soul which reveals itself in the thoughts and actions which emerge. There may be opportunities to fly high spiritually but they are tempered by the practical commitments of human life. All religions teach that the absolutely sublime is found in the absolutely ordinary; we only need to look closely at nature for proof of this.

Secondly, regardless of the extent to which we feed the spirit, it continues to try to carry out its roles of promoting our uniqueness, maintaining our integrity and seeking opportunities for spiritual growth. However, if we fail to nourish it, it has less scope to perform its roles. Thus, if we want the benefits of spiritual living, we have to spend time in nurturing the soul so that it can mull over the happenings of everyday life, identify the issues for us, discover the sources of pain and suffering and provide us with guidance and joy. Often this is about finding space for the soul to do its work. Only when we step back from our self-concern, can we see the enlarged notion of what it means to be human; only by making sacrifices of time or money do we chip away at our selfishness; only by making space can we experience the things that are beyond our knowledge and control.

Thirdly, the things that feed the soul most directly are the things of the spirit, the things which give us deep pleasure and solace, such as humour, beauty, music, image, courage, family, intimacy, memory, sensation, art and atmosphere - you might identify other things. If we are to increase our exposure to these things, we may need to change the way we live. For example, our homes and workplaces may need to be adjusted to allow the spiritual to speak to us.

The soul is on the look out, keeping us awake and alert. It receives signals from the spiritual world. It is iterating and refining, providing us with vision and energy, transforming us where necessary; this is a deepening process as we are enabled to recognise complexity, identify beauty, pursue justice, work to make the world a truly colourful and passionate place; the deepening comes through intuition and imagination, impressions and sensations, diversity and individuality, richness and pleasure.

So, if we want a more fulfilled and meaningful life, we have to train ourselves to allow the spirit in. Such training involves a range of activities:

- we have to learn to detach ourselves from whatever occupies our minds to excess (perhaps making money, perhaps our membership of a club, perhaps physical pursuits) so that we can focus on other things; non-attachment is a state recommended by all the main religions;
- we have to learn to live with mystery and uncertainty so that we are able to appreciate amazing and wondrous sights, sounds, ideas, images that come from outside our regular experience; they are to be respected and studied;
- we have to learn to stop filling our lives with action and ideas and be willing to simply wait quietly and patiently for the spirit to come to us in new visions, ideas, dreams and images; this is about becoming comfortable with silence and emptiness because it is only when we make space that the spirit can shine into our lives and our soul can respond;
- we have to stop worrying about our well-being and be prepared to put our trust in the world in which we live to care for us;
- we have to learn to recognise our own limitations whilst appreciating more fully the contributions of others; this strengthens us as we become more honest with ourselves and more enlightened.
- we have to learn that there is ancient wisdom in life, in others, in the world.

The more we do these things, the more the soul is able to guide us through our lives because we are giving it space to do its work. It will offer us new opportunities as we trust more, worry less, let things happen to us, become more relaxed and stop thinking that we always have to be in control. We will receive greater awareness and depth so that we know things even when we do not fully understand everything.

All of this involves us in being open to change and we will be open if we start to see people and places as belonging to the spirit rather than to people. The world is still around because most of our ancestors saw it as belonging not to them but to all humans and animals that have ever existed and that will ever exist. People were generally grateful for the care that their predecessors had taken with the gift of the world and felt responsible for preserving the world for their successors. There was a strong sense of the spiritual and eternal and people saw themselves as guardians of a world given to them to care for. Because they were closer to the land and to nature in their daily work, they were alive to wonder at the amazing things in the natural world that they were caring for, and they were grateful. In the main they were compassionate in their dealings with their fellow human beings and animals who shared the planet and they sought justice for all. They recognised the unusual abilities given to human beings that allowed them to pursue knowledge and freedom, and they gave priority to being in a relationship with the spirit who they saw as the creator and giver of all good things.

Once human beings began to think that the earth belonged to them to use as they saw fit for short-term ends, they started to lose the plot, both as individuals and as a species. Destructive use of our planet has grown out of proportion in the last hundred years and many people have lost a sense of perspective about ownership and continuity. They no longer respect all that has been achieved in the past and care less about the needs of those who will follow. Such people seem to have ceased to be open to eternal values and they focus on short-term money-making which is a symbol of our secular age. They are no longer open to the wonders and glories of the planet on which we are located

A few practical points

Let us finish with a few practical ways of feeding the soul; some of them will be followed up in more detail in the next few chapters.

Probably the most effective form of nourishment is becoming more attentive. The first stage in this is to develop our capacity to listen – to listen to others who want us to hear what they are saying, to listen to those who are in need and are wanting our help and to listen to the world which is full of the spirit. The second is to use our other senses (sight, touch, smell, taste) to become more aware of the world around us and all its wonderful aspects. By living closer to nature and more attentively, we can start to enjoy silence and develop our sense of wonder. By getting rid of the clutter and lack of focus in our lives, by removing our self-concern and preoccupation with our own agendas, we will start to see so much more. We do this by seeing each experience and moment as uniquely important. Thus the people and situations that we encounter demand our conscious awareness and our full attention so that we allow things, people and experiences to speak for themselves. We can then make our actions, choices and judgments in line with our spiritual understanding. Buddhism teaches attentiveness as listening deeply (respectfully, with willingness to change), listening quietly (to things all around one), looking deeply at nature and art, and being awake to see the evidence of the spirit's love all around – for example, in a smile, an embrace, a letter or a flower.

Related to increased attentiveness is keeping close to our roots. We need to value more highly the things that are around us all the time, the gifts of nature and people (including those who have gone before), and draw energy from them. Living close to the spirit involves us in identifying with the needs of the world and seeking to pursue the spiritual outcome wherever we live and work. So we feed the soul by attending to detail, caring for family and friends, being sensitive to the importance of home, daily work, the clothes we wear, the food we eat, and so on. There are many ways in which we can enhance our approach to these ordinary aspects of life, for example, by analysing from time to time what works for us and what doesn't, by taking walks instead of driving, keeping the television switched off except for special programmes, installing some artwork at home, working together to choose colour schemes, eating meals around a family table, sharing together in games or live entertainment. You will be able to think of many other examples.

How many of us take time out – to listen, to watch, to read, to sit quietly, to enjoy silence, to spend time with close family and friends, to look carefully at the beauty of nature as it manifests itself all around us. In my experience not enough of us do. We see ourselves as trapped on a never-ending tread-mill leading us nowhere other than to maintain our so-called standard of living. People spend more time working than ever before; husbands and wives work and see less and less of each other; and much of our leisure can be spent on unedifying pursuits such as watching uninspiring television programmes, drinking heavily and wasting money on short-lived pleasures. If we want to get off the tread-mill, we can do so. It simply requires the courage to move away from the material domination of our lives and to embrace more fully the spiritual dimension. This involves deciding that more and more possessions are unnecessary and that a simpler life style provides all the pleasures that human existence offers. Such a change brings about more balance in the way we live because we refuse to allow the short-term and material to dominate our lives. What a release! How will we use the time?

The soul is nurtured by beauty and lack of it causes dysfunction. Beauty is arresting, it takes you out of the day-to-day into the eternal realm (e.g. a sudden vista, a painting, a film, an artefact). Beauty is a quality of people or things or ideas which are absorbing, invite contemplation and stimulate the imagination. Beauty is necessary for the soul's functioning. We need exposure to music, art, food, landscapes, cultures and climates and they should influence our lives. Art is an important part of life wherever we are; it should not be divorced from daily living and put in a gallery or museum. Where we live has an influence on our soul and vice versa; so cleaning the plates, scrubbing the floors, choosing wallpaper, decorating the Christmas tree, creating a warm environment etc. are all ways of cherishing it. Similarly in the office or the club, indeed anywhere where we spend a lot of time, what you sit on, what you look at, whom you work with affect your feelings and your soul. Spiritual resources are to be found in special places, beautiful objects, stunning scenery, the design of a product, the courage of a friend.

Finally, spiritual writers have often taught being spiritual begins with compassionate seeing: "The more you see of people, the more you will love them". As we walk through our streets and public places, go to supermarkets, or travel on the bus or train, we can look deeply at people with the eyes of the spirit. Nourishment of our soul is not just for ourselves; we receive the spiritual perspective in order to bless others; we are to pass on the spirit's love and compassion to others because we have experienced it ourselves.

Some points to consider

1. Having read the previous chapter and this one, are you happy with the idea of a soul? If not, try to identify the reasons for your unease.
2. Consider the requirements for a fully functioning soul and identify any which seem unnecessary or any which you feel are missing. Do you agree with the list of things that stop the soul from performing well?
3. Do the three blockages to soul growth make sense to you? Are there other things that might stand in the way of soul growth?
4. In the light of the discussion of nourishing the soul and the practical points, can you produce a checklist of behaviours that you might try to embrace in your life in order to feed your soul and enhance your spiritual understanding of life?

5. What can we learn about spirituality from religions?

Some people would say that the most obvious way in which spirituality expresses itself is through religion. There are three definitions of the word 'religion' in the Oxford English Dictionary: "human recognition of superhuman controlling power, and especially of a personal God entitled to obedience"; "effect of such recognition on conduct and mental attitude", and "one of the prevalent systems of faith and worship". The first two are inter-related and articulate the human response to the sacred which is at the heart of religion, whereas the third is narrower, relating to the institutional form that particular religions take. Religion as "the human response to the sacred" (the first two of our definitions) involves human beings' sense of the numinous, experience of depth, ultimate meaning and inexhaustible mystery, and feeling of being under obligation (which leads to righteousness, piety, authentic engagement with the world and a disciplined way of living). These are elements of the spirituality which underpins and shapes a religion in its institutional form.

To avoid including a discussion of each of the major religions in this chapter an Appendix gives a brief summary of Hinduism, Buddhism, Confucianism/Taoism, Judaism, Christianity and Islam under six headings:

- a brief history
- beliefs/response to the sacred

- scriptures and theology
- practices, rituals and ceremonies
- the search for higher truth
- structure and organisation.

Please turn to the Appendix now, if you need a short description of any or all of them.

How did religions come about?

This is a difficult question to answer. Some would say that human beings are naturally religious, but, if you accept my definition of religion as institutionalised spirituality, it is clear that many people are not naturally religious; they may be naturally spiritual but that does not lead them to follow a specific set of beliefs and participate in a particular structure that a religion defines.

Some would argue that religions come about because God reveals himself in a particular way (e.g. to Gautama, to Lao, to Moses, to Jesus, to Muhammad, and so on) with a particular specification of how he is to be worshipped (note that it is always a man who receives the revelation and that the God is usually male!). The trouble with this explanation is that it is only true for the particular religion with the particular revelation; it is not true for all religions.

Some suggest that religious belief stems from man's fear of the unknown. The difficulty with this explanation is that the unknown is becoming more and more known but still many thousands of people turn to religion day by day. Even if we think about our early ancestors, we find that they coped with the unknown much better than we may have imagined, They certainly were not afraid of death as they believed in an after-life; they buried people with food and useful equipment for the next life; and they, almost without exception, held their ancestors in awe and paid respect to them in a way that many people find strange today. Clearly they thought about death and had a strong desire to survive but they knew that they would die and this does not seem so much to have frightened them as to have encouraged them to believe in life after death. Humans differ from animals in being aware of death and being able to think beyond the immediate.

Setting aside those explanations, perhaps we can turn to some suggestions that seem to me to be more tenable. The first might be that the religious impulse stems from wonder at and respect for the rhythms of the natural world. When so-called primitive people were asked by researchers how their religious ideas developed they almost all reported that the things that they regarded as sacred came from observation of the created world. The cycles, patterns and order which early humans observed could not be attributed to mankind or the animals. So they explained it as due to superhuman and supernatural powers, who were worthy of worship, especially if by this means they could be influenced to make life less difficult for the worshippers. Today people in general are in awe of the natural cycle even though science is finding explanations for many of the things that have previously amazed us.

Linked to this possible explanation is the sense of responsibility, which our ancestors felt keenly but which many of us today seem to have lost, that they were obliged by those who had come before them and by those who would come after them to preserve the world in as good a condition as they could. At very least they should not make it worse for those who come next. After all they had benefited from the care which their predecessors had given to the world in which they lived. This set of beliefs was strong, especially in the days when humans hunted for food and later when agriculture took over; people felt a sense of awe, respect and reverence for what they had been given and believed that whoever gave it to them should be worshipped. Thus scholars of religion and mythology show us that the development of religious ideas moved through four periods which overlapped in different places: when animals were the main source of food, powerful animals were the object of worship; when mankind started to grow food, sun and rain and fertility became the dominant forces; as food became more secure, astronomers studied the sky to predict seasons and weather patterns and discovered a cosmic order which led to other systems of belief; and finally as human beings began to realise their own powers of thought and creativity the focus moved to the spirit within.

A third source of religious thinking might be concern for others, especially those in need. Although our animal nature is as deeply ingrained as in other animals (e.g. "eat or be eaten"), humans seem to have always felt a need to suspend their desire for self-preservation when they see another person in danger; we seem to have an innate desire to protect each other. Perhaps humans have an inherent sense of unity because they share the same type of life, and this may be another driving force for the religious instinct.

Another reason for religious belief might be the widespread disinclination, even today, to believe in chance or accident as the prevailing life force. People prefer to believe that things happen by design because they put all their ingenuity and effort into designing their own future, in whatever form it takes. You have to believe that what you are doing is leading in the direction that you want in order to keep going; similarly there is a strong inclination to believe that there is a grand design behind the created world so that we can make sense of life.

A fifth explanation that has some credibility for me is the argument of mystery. We all know that life is subject to factors beyond human control; even scientists today are increasingly coming to that conclusion. We live in a world which cannot be fully defined, even though our knowledge of it is becoming greater each day. It is a world in which creativity, ingenuity and genius cannot be pinned down; they are a gift in which we should all rejoice. The world has lots of mysteries which cannot be explained; nor should we want to explain everything. This leads people to place their trust in mystery believing that it is underpinned by a benign force.

A sixth suggestion derives from the human beings that we call today shamans, people who are able through trances, visions and ecstatic states to contact the spirit world and return with insights into the supernatural that cannot be rationalised but which are for many who receive them completely understandable and true. Such gifted individuals have occurred in all generations and have been greatly respected. Even today, in our cynical western society, there remain many who will vouch for the validity and sincerity of such experiences.

The final plausible explanation for religious belief is the one discussed in chapter 2 – the fact that we all have some sense of the numinous, the sacred, the transcendent. We have experiences that inspire a sense of wonder, of being in the presence of something outside of ourselves. Such experiences are mysterious and wondrous; some, like a bolt of lightning, may inspire us with a sense of terror but they fill us with awe and fascination and a desire to draw closer to the source. Such experiences, together with the human desire to reason about life, are sources of the interest in religion.

In conclusion, we can perhaps attribute the origin of religion to the side of human life which gives us the ability to think for ourselves, to look for order in our surroundings, to want to make sense of life and to desire keenly to survive, and which offers us experience of the sacred, awe-inspiring and transcendent such that we have a sense of being dependent on powers greater than ourselves.

Religious belief

All religions involve belief. Let us consider what that means. We speak of belief in at least four different ways: as believing an idea when we accept an argument (e.g. believing a scientific argument); as believing a person (e.g. believing Jim Smith) when we mean that we believe that he is speaking the truth; as believing a theory when we give overall assent to it (e.g. believing in democracy as a political system); and as believing in a person (e.g. I believe in my son) when we are committing ourselves to supporting them. The common feature of these ways of speaking is we are making a commitment (whether intellectual, emotional or ideological) to whatever it is that we believe; this is a commitment of the heart as well as of the mind because we can never be totally certain of anything. So when people ask me 'what do you believe?' I tend to answer that I am committed to an overall explanation of life along the lines of this book and that as far as possible this influences/drives all that I do and say. In other words I have a world-view or metaphor of life which I hold dear and which guides me, as explained in chapter 3. In a similar sense, when Christians say the creed in an act of worship, most are not proclaiming an intellectual belief in the factual truth of the statements but are committing themselves to the world-view represented by the words.

Usually religious belief means belief in a particular religion and this is in the main culturally determined. This is not necessarily a bad thing so long as the religion does not claim exclusivity and seek to convert (sometimes by violence) those who do not subscribe to it. The more tenable position now that we have so much more knowledge of religion is a pluralist one, in which a person from any one religion can feel a deep fellow feeling with those from another. There is a rich diversity in the various religions and we are seeing boundaries being softened as elements of one become components of another. All religions need a pluralist outlook which is less dogmatic and more exploratory, less exclusive and more open, less specific and more holistic, less negative and more positive. The challenge for religious institutions is to help people to see that they live work and play in a sacred space and that holy places are not just for devotional worship but also for reflection, conversation and spiritual direction. Demands for conformity and exclusivity seem to me to be completely out of place in this aim. Atheists and sceptics often have greater depth to their beliefs, because they have thought things through and have a compelling world-view, than those who trust in dogma and discipline. Belief is commitment to a world-view (embracing it with affection if not love) but there is no room for intolerance. Very often those without religious belief are committed to a caring and compassionate way of living which puts to shame those who make such a profession but spend their time excluding and criticising.

Religious faith

In the context of religion, faith is a word sometimes used instead of belief. Some think that faith is simply unquestioning belief which they think is naïve and irrational. On the contrary, faith is more like a world-view. Faith is the word which is used to describe how people centre their lives on a spiritual understanding of the world, embracing life in all its fullness and accepting uncertainty and mystery without reservation, as they come to know who they are.

Thus faith is a dynamic process of developing an explanation of life. Think of how, when a scientist looks under a microscope at a globule of water; s/he sees a whole world of life in continuous movement, whereas when we non-scientists look all we can see is a globule of water; the scientist knows what s/he is looking at. A person of faith can see a meaning and purpose to life which other people cannot see. Just as an artist can look at something quite ordinary like an urn or a bowl of fruit and use his/her art to point us to a higher reality, so a person of faith has a clear idea of eternal values.

Faith is a journey without end; it continues to question, to wonder and to experience uncertainty as it explores life and is stirred by the soul. It is a unique journey for each one of us since no-one has trodden our path before us, though of course we can learn from others. Faith involves trust in a world-view that makes increasing sense as we experience life. It is a commitment to something which cannot be scientifically proved or demonstrated and so it is vulnerable (because there is the possibility that the trust may be betrayed) but it is strong and capable of surviving.

Such faith is grounded in real life. Those who live in a bubble of belief which is entirely divorced from day-to-day living find themselves unable to trust in life. They use their belief system to keep the world at a distance and are less able to respond to unusual or different or unexpected events.

Religious practice

We can learn a lot about deepening our spiritual life by looking at religious practice and experience. All religions share an emphasis on the importance of stories, rituals, buildings, art, music, prayer, and places of pilgrimage

Stories (or myths or metaphors) provide us with a means for setting aside the particularities of personal and social differences so that we can learn lessons about the great issues of human existence. They are based on types of people rather than actual people (though, of course, actual people are the foundation for the type). The study of myths (mythology) brings them together to reveal patterns of human thinking and behaving which encourage us to reflect on life. They help us towards insights; they are not to be taken literally; they simply reach beyond the limits of our ordinary human lives to recognise eternal truths.

Stories and ritual are closely connected. Rituals encourage us to think through the significance of major stages in human life by developing ways and words for celebration or commiseration. They help us to engage but they do not necessarily make sense in a literal context; if we think of a baptism or a wedding, much use is made of symbols (e.g. water, rings) to convey meaning rather than literal truth. We do not wed with a ring; we use the ring to speak of the eternity of love or the binding together of two hearts. Ritual and the objects and images that it uses are very important in our everyday life as well as religious and social life. The positions in which we sit at table for a meal, the table cloth that is used, the crockery brought out for special occasions all carry meaning and communicate feelings to those familiar with them. These are objects and actions that may have little effect on daily life but speak loudly to our spiritual life. Key rituals in religions reflect the religion's interpretation of how life should be lived and they feed the soul.

In all religions iconography, art and architecture speak to us about spirituality. In Christianity, the mediaeval cathedrals are monuments to the way people thought about the religious life. The high steeple and gothic windows point towards heaven, the carved images of saints are intended to be exemplars for the congregation, the beautiful stained glass windows provide images from the scriptures for the benefit of those who were unable to read. The person entering the cathedral was to be confronted by grandeur on a magnificent scale so as to be drawn in awe towards worship of the almighty. The robes of the priests established their senior position in the hierarchy. The tombs, chapels and crypts were signs of the faith of the wealthy aristocracy who endowed the cathedral and a reminder to the ordinary people of the status quo which the church endorsed. Today when one enters a magnificent cathedral or even a local parish church, one can sense something of the important themes in religious spirituality: quietness for prayer, darkness for internal reflection, strong images to stimulate the imagination, stories of the faith told by windows, carvings and paintings for contemplation. It is not surprising that the cathedrals became centres of pilgrimage because they reinforced the faith so well, especially if, as they usually were, they were located in a holy place where a committed believer had been martyred for his or her faith.

Similarly, the music of religions has a strong role in reinforcing the faith. The beauty of the music is uplifting; the words of the hymns tell the stories of the faith; the learning of doctrine is made easier with rhythm; the themes of sin and repentance, grace and mercy, death and resurrection are taught.

Similarities and differences in the major religions

You will find in the Appendix on the major religions that the "the human response to the sacred" is expressed in religions through beliefs, some form of scripture and theological doctrine, ritual, prayer, sacrifice, pilgrimage, art and symbolism, temples, churches, mosques, codes of morality and conduct, and systems of justice which extend into life beyond death.

There are many similarities in the religions. They all are concerned with experience of a dimension beyond our material and temporal world. The sacredness arises from objects, places or experiences which lead people to feel the presence of someone or something outside of themselves which is mysterious, compelling or beautiful. Religions promote or respond to a sense of reality beyond the immediately visible which for believers is important and lasting and arouses awe. They involve belief in a being or

71

beings, or a force, or something beyond definition, which gives meaning to life; often this is described as a supreme, unchanging, eternal reality.

The belief is usually in one or more gods whom the adherents worship in various ways, often based on some form of scripture; these are interpreted into rules governing behaviour, usually related to a system of justice which extends to life beyond death; they are reinforced by rites and rituals, often related to the human life-cycle; they encourage adherents to pray, to fast, to make sacrifices, to give to those in need, to visit holy shrines and to reflect on their spiritual life; they organise themselves through physical (e.g. temples, mosques, churches) and human (e.g. priests, monks, presbyters, imams, rabbis) structures; and they are sources of creativity, art and symbolism.

All religions seem to have groups which are more positive in their view of humanity, emphasising the good, the joyful and the value of human life, and groups which are more negative, emphasising the evil, the miserable and sinful side of human nature. Also all religions seem to have a higher version, which is pursued by an elite of philosophical intellectuals, who are concerned with ways of reaching union with their god, and a lower version which is more down to earth and practical and concerned with obtaining security and material wealth and warding off evil by securing the good will of the supernatural power(s) in whose hands good things lie.

If we look at words which are used by the various religions to express aspects of the religious way of life, we find frequent references to:

- Love, compassion and caring
- Gentleness, tolerance, non-violence and peace

- Renunciation of selfishness and worldliness
- Purity and asceticism
- Truth, trust and honesty
- Benevolence, respect and doing good
- Justice and fair dealing
- Generosity and hospitality
- Wisdom and meditation
- Caring for outcasts and the poor.

These give us a good indication of the spirituality which underpins religions.

There are also major differences <u>between</u> the religions, especially in relation to how they see the purpose of life and the means of salvation, and their emphasis on winning converts. The eastern religions (Hinduism, Buddhism and Taoism) are more tolerant and pluralistic than the western; they allow for a range of routes to the truth. There are wide differences in ideas of what a god is (ranging through animals, trees, the forces of wind or rain or sun, ancestors, saints, larger-than-life individuals, life-force, eternal father and/or mother to vast impersonal energy) and where a god is located. There are differences in the extent to which the feminine is present among the gods and in the extent to which the animal world is respected as part of the sacredness of all life. Finally, there are considerable differences in emphasis in relation to the role of religion in community life, the treatment of sin and the extent to which a god operates within a person

Also there are differences <u>within</u> religions in terms of the number of sects/denominations, different styles of worship and internal contradictions.

Thus they have the same root in the human desire for a sense of purpose, unity and discipline, and in religious experience but they offer very different answers. Some writers group religions into two main types:

1. **Religions of the wheel** (Buddhism and Hinduism, for example) see life as a journey around the rim of a wheel which is continuously rotating around a motionless centre. Human beings follow an endless cycle, to which the soul returns in different forms, of birth, death and re-birth as they journey round the perimeter of the wheel. The way to salvation is to escape from the rim to the hub (where God is, in the form of motionless peace) and various spokes can be used as routes to the hub (e.g. the teachings of holy men and prophets, scriptures etc.), as in this illustration.

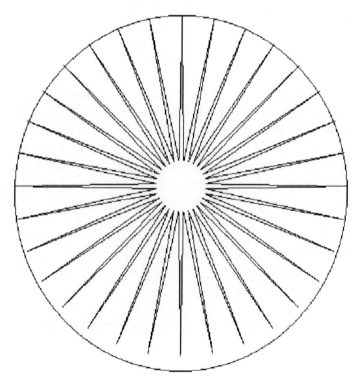

2. **Religions of the road** (Judaism, Islam, Christianity), on the other hand, see life as a once-off journey towards a goal which has been revealed by God. All three believe that meaning is to be found in a future consummation and they all share the concept of one God and the Old Testament, but beyond that are quite different. Judaism is a religion of common descent, not interested in converting people. Islam advocates the fulfilment of God's will through community, in which ritual, personal relationships, business affairs, government are ruled by divinely inspired law. Christianity has an ideal of fellowship in Jesus Christ, receiving the Holy Spirit, with a mission to the world.

William James in his far reaching study of world religions[2] identified four key similarities: all religions are concerned with enabling human beings to express their experience of the sacred; they provide routes for personal and social spiritual growth; they contain a rich diversity of religious practice; and they result in changed behaviour. On the other hand he found one area of major difference - in their beliefs and doctrines, which are, of course, most affected by culture and language. Religions, especially their scriptures, doctrines, teachings and rituals, were developed by human beings through creative and imaginative thinking about the sacred. Thus they reflect the social and cultural context in which they came into being and they use its language; over time the religions themselves become part of the culture.

Religions then bring to us storehouses of wisdom from the past offering us a view of what is important in life and how we ought to live and aesthetic traditions whose music, poetry, stories, art, architecture, worship and ritual

2   William James, "The Varieties of Religious Experience", Penguin, London 1983

reveal the sacred to us. They also provide vehicles for living the religious life and engaging in spiritual practices and encourage people and society to become less selfish and more compassionate. All of these features are concerned with helping human beings to develop a transforming relationship with God, the sacred, the other.

Secularism

Let us now turn to the ways in which the world, especially in the west, has been changing over the past 100 years and how secularism has gained ground. Secularism is defined as a way of interpreting life, organising and behaving without reference to religion.

Firstly, science has given us new perspectives on life on earth (in terms of cosmology, evolution, ecology, bio-science, medical science), insights into human behaviour (through psychology, sociology and economics) and much greater availability of information (through information and communications technology); consequently the world-view which underpins the major religions is considered anachronistic.

Secondly, despite scientific developments and increased knowledge, there is a consensus that the world has become more fragmented, cruel and violent (the past century saw among other things two world wars, the development and use of weapons of mass destruction, the holocaust, ethnic cleansing, international terrorism, reluctance to tackle poverty, hunger and disease among the poorer nations despite huge increases in wealth in the west); the traditional message of an intervening and omnipotent God has lost its relevance for many people.

Thirdly, as wealth has increased in the west, people have become more self-centred, competitive and individualistic, driven by consumerism and instrumentalism, feeling emancipated yet alienated and disempowered, measuring success in largely material terms; lives have become more superficial and there is less sense of community.

Fourthly and more recently, western democracies have experienced an upsurge of people asserting their rights, especially to "do their own thing"; this has been accompanied by a rejection of traditional authority, unwillingness to trust in absolutes, and strong emphasis on personal independence; there has been a reaction against institutions like the churches as irrelevant and organised religion as unnecessary; people are cutting themselves off from traditional beliefs which gave meaning, purpose and value to ordinary lives. Countries that once saw religious unity as a political priority no longer do so and religion has become a private matter; many are pleased by this (both religious and non-religious) but there is a general concern that the decline of religion has led to a weakening in the fabric of society; something good has been lost. However, when authors write of religion being in decline, they are referring usually to its institutional form rather than the human response to the sacred.

These developments have for many people cast severe doubt on the religious interpretation of human life and as a result there are strong movements, especially in the west, to remove religion from social structures and political life. These movements are known collectively as secularism.

New age pick-and-mix spirituality

For fifteen centuries the west largely accepted the Christian understanding of God and his dealings with human beings. This was challenged by the Enlightenment's emphasis on individuality and individual responsibility, which resulted in competing denominations/traditions with very different understandings of God. God and the church, however, remained important for most people until relatively recently. Now religious institutions have become for many a hindrance to seeking a more spiritual life. Interest in the sacred, the mysterious and the ultimate has not declined but is less closely linked to clearly defined belief-systems. We live in a world of choices and preferences, in which people seek their own meaningful lifestyles. In this world, spiritualities are products to be chosen. This is suited to the current age in which personal autonomy is stressed; it encourages exploration, affirms the importance of experience and welcomes the challenges of pluralism; but it can be individualistic and self-seeking, limited to the inner life with a weak ethical base, insufficiently concerned with daily living and others' needs; also it can be more about "what can people get out of the spirit" rather than what can they give.

In this context people, mainly in the west, are turning towards an incoherent collection of practices which helps them to meet some of their spiritual needs. This is sometimes known as new age pick-and-mix spirituality. Some of the techniques which are advertised locally under the heading of new age spirituality include: Aromatherapy, Art therapy, Astrology, Buddhist meditation, Chiropractice, Circle Dancing, Flower essences therapy, Foot massage, Herbalism, Homeopathy, Hypnotherapy, Indian head massage, Massage, Palm readings, Psychic consultancy, Psychotherapy, Rebirthing, Reflexology, Reiki, Relaxation therapy, Shiatsu, Spiritual healing, Tai Chi/Chi Kung, Tarot, Universal Peace dancing group and Yoga. Some of these belong more appropriately under the heading alternative medicine but it is interesting that they are seen by the providers as being part of new age spirituality. Perhaps it is a good marketing brand at the moment.

There seem to be three approaches to new age spirituality. First, there are those who purchase stand-alone practices/ techniques which they think will help them spiritually; some of these are in the list above and they are sold as packaged courses with no necessary relationship to their source (e.g. yoga as a fitness technique rather than as a practice of spiritual awareness in the context of Hindu beliefs). Second, there are those who are seeking deeper spiritual awareness and are eclectic in their choice of practices (i.e. not using the particular offerings of a particular religion but drawing on a pluralist model), seeing a particular practice (e.g. meditation) as having intrinsic spiritual value. Third, there are those who belong to a particular religion and have found a practice, perhaps from another sect or denomination, such as Benedictine or Ignatian spirituality within Christianity, and make use of the spiritual practice within a framework of beliefs.

The separation of religion and spirituality is relatively recent, a western emphasis; in the east today and throughout most of history they have been intertwined, human spirituality giving rise to religion and religion expressing its spirituality in a variety of practices. Both are part of a faithful response to the sacred and the ultimate and involve disciplined practices, inner depth, authentic engagement with the world, mystery of immanence and transcendence, and emphasis on the non-material aspects of existence. They differ in that institutional religion tends to be associated with form and organisation (ritual, worship, creed, cosmology, buildings, unconditional devotion, membership, community and conformity) whereas spirituality tends to be associated with individual freedom and growth (eclecticism, holism, solitude, experience, personal ownership, cultural commitment). In the west there is evidence that people are exercising their right to choose those elements of various religions that they believe are helpful to them.

Some points to consider

1. Seven possible explanations are given for the development of religions. Which do you feel are the more likely – and why?

2. From your knowledge of religions (perhaps aided by the Appendix) does the discussion of similarities and differences seem adequate to you or would you emphasise other points?

3. Does the discussion of religious belief and religious faith help you to understand how religious people think? Is a world-view a good way of explaining religious faith?

4. Drawing from your knowledge of religious practice can you identify the elements which contribute most to spiritual growth?

5. Some religions feel threatened by secularism. Do you feel that this feeling is justified? Why?

6. What is your experience of so-called New Age Spirituality? Does it have spiritual depth?

PART 2

Dimensions of spiritual living

6. Living together and in community

The spiritual understanding of life starts with relationship and connectedness. It has a world-view that sees the purpose of human life as being caring for the world and its people so that those who follow us can enjoy the privilege of living here to the same extent as we have. This involves recognising what we have inherited from others and ensuring that we leave a world that is better than the one which we entered. We do this by caring and caring involves those around us – our family, our friends, our neighbours, our fellow citizens and those far away who make up the world population – as well as for the world in which we live. Each of us in our behaviour is like a stone dropping into a pool; we create ripples that move outwards to other people who are affected by the things that we say or do. Our spiritual responsibility is to ensure that we are caring for and building up those who are in relationship with us.

Living together

The spirit may seem to some to be an abstract idea but its role is anything but abstract. It is the spirit which encourages humans to love one another and look after the world. You cannot be a spiritual person or have a spiritual understanding of life without concrete involvement with your neighbours and community. How we relate to others is a fundamental part of our spirituality. It is not possible to be spiritual on one's own, although at times being alone is essential to charging the spiritual batteries. Being spiritual is about being involved with other people, who may be close at hand (in the family or living nearby) or far afield, even on the other side of the world. During our existence on earth we share it with all those who are simultaneously alive and so we have an obligation to be concerned for them and them for us. Of course, we cannot have close dealings with huge numbers of people but it is surprising how closely people are related. Recent research on texts and emails has revealed that each individual is only six relationships away from being in contact with every person on the planet. In simple terms the mathematics support this: say you have contact with two hundred persons (not an unreasonable number for each individual especially in the developed world) and each of them has contact with 200 people, that means that, through your 200 relationships, you are potentially in touch with $200 \times 200 = 40,000$ people; if we halve each set of contacts to allow for overlaps, it becomes to 10,000, and if each of them has 100 non-overlapping contacts we arrive at 1 million; if we continue to extrapolate in the same way through four more sets of contacts, we arrive at 10 trillion people, well in excess of the world population. Of course, these calculations make huge assumptions that you may wish to question but they are indicative of the 'smallness' of the world as it now is.

The reason that involvement in a concrete way with other people is essential to spirituality is that it is through people that our spirituality is mainly exercised. It is other people who both contribute to the enrichment of our soul and confront or challenge our thinking about life. We cannot believe in caring for people without putting it into practice. Theory without practice is meaningless; it allows us to make all sorts of claims and develop fanciful notions of our own connectedness; it is only by putting the theory into practice that we learn and develop. It is through others that our false ideas about ourselves are tested and our soul helps us to a firmer understanding of who we are. Thus being spiritual is not a private matter, being human is not a private matter;

both are expressed through other people and the ways in which we treat other living creatures and the resources of our world.

An illustration which is often used to explain this is shown

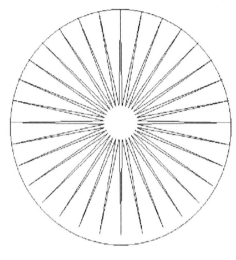

here. The idea is that if you regard people as travelling towards the spirit they can be represented by spokes of a wheel. You will note that as you move closer to the spirit, so you move closer to other people; you cannot move closer to people unless you move closer to the spirit and you cannot move closer to the spirit unless you move closer to other people.

When we are born, we come into the world as one person among many; we are not on our own; if we were, we could not survive since we are dependent on others to feed, clothe and teach us. As we go through life we learn how to relate to others and psychologists tell us that the more loving the people around us as we grow the more likely it is that we will want to show the same love to others. However we all go through periods, especially in adolescence, of wanting to be different, wanting to be individual. As we mature we return to a greater realisation of our interdependence and we seek to fulfil our calling of building up human life in and through others. We are called to care for and help one another.

It is also worth noting how little we can achieve alone (though the contributions of a few exceptional people challenge this idea); most change is brought about by individuals coming together and persuading others to move in a particular direction or take a shared decision. Even those in positions of great power have to win people over to their way of thinking; otherwise resentment will occur and sooner or later this spells disaster. By working together people can achieve huge change.

Ourselves and others

Our spiritual life is revealed in our daily living. Perhaps we find it easy to love our close family (though some people find even this difficult) but our commitment to the spirit sends us towards those who are not members of our family and we are to love them too. Again some people find this difficult perhaps because they have lost something of the closeness and sharing with neighbours these days. There are many reasons (increased personal wealth, changed lifestyles because of television and the car, changed working patterns, etc.) but this just means that we need to find new ways of caring for one another. The love which we experience is not simply to be shared with those whom we like and know well, but with all people whom we rub up against in life – the man who lives next to us and perhaps plays the same music at too high a volume every day; the woman who sits at the next desk who never stops chattering; the youngster who keeps kicking his ball into our garden, and so on – these are the people we are challenged to love. It is easy to love our family or friends, but it is much more difficult to love those with whom we have few ties.

Family life, however defined, has proved to be a lasting and effective vehicle for human beings to find personal closeness, to achieve economic stability and to rear children. It reflects the family groupings that we find in the animal kingdom but it has been carried to a higher plane by human beings in terms of intimacy, trust, mutual dependence and friendship. There is little doubt that the marriage/partnership of two people who have found a loving, caring, respecting relationship leads to healthier, more stable and happier lives and this is the ideal situation for children to grow up in. Recent trends in the break-up of marriages in the western world are not good for children in particular but it is not possible to go back because the world has changed and traditional roles (e.g. of mothers being at home with their children) cannot easily be resurrected. Nonetheless a spiritual understanding of life sees strength in the family and seeks to build it up, in whatever form it finds it. Thus keeping in contact with brothers and sisters and their children, looking after aging relatives and continuing to support your children as they move on are desirable activities and energy should be devoted to them.

Friendship is surely one of the most important elements of the spiritual life, whether considered in terms of good company, a shared meal or a frank conversation or on a higher plane in terms of trust and sacrifice. Friendships enrich our lives and contribute to our happiness, thus feeding the soul. Friendship was seen in the ancient world to be the purest form of love between humans and this noble idea of friendship passed into western culture through the writings of Aristotle, Cicero and Augustine. Religions have seen friendship as a route to knowledge of God. A mediaeval priest, later saint, Aelred wrote[3] that there was "nothing more sacred … nothing more useful … nothing more difficult … nothing more sweet … and nothing more profitable" than friendship. He saw friendship as a means of combating loneliness, heightening joys, and mitigating

---

3   Aelred of Rievaulx, "Spiritual Friendship", Cistercian Publica-
      tions, US, 1989, p.72

sorrow. He wrote that friendship provides support and security, someone to confess to and someone to share burdens, doubts and plans with, without fear of criticism, correction or suspicion.

I describe friendship as an element of the spiritual life because at its core is the sharing of love. Yet friendship seems more difficult to enter into in our age than it was previously. For some people this is because of long working hours, for others it stems from the reduced amount of time given to hospitality, for others it is a reflection of some modern ways of thinking in which relationships are seen as instrumental, and for yet others the obligations of friendship are too pressing. There is no doubt that a true friendship makes demands on time, attention, caring, loyalty, patience and vulnerability but those who give these things to it believe that they are greatly rewarded. Friendship is a gift which is worth nurturing.

Most of us like to have friends of the kind described above and we seek them out in places where people come together, e.g. school, work, church, club, pub. In the past our neighbours might have been our friends because we saw more of them than other people. For some that remains the case but in our world of greater mobility, increased leisure and longer working hours, people find their friends in other places. Nonetheless our immediate neighbours are important to our lives because of their physical proximity and there is a strong obligation for the spiritual person to seek out and support those near at hand as well as those further afield.

Living in community

People come together in communities because together they can achieve much more than they can as individuals. We are often told that when geese fly together in a flock they can achieve 70% greater distance than they can when alone and when they fly in formation (usually a V shape to increase the updraught of air) they can fly 75% further than a single goose alone. With humans it is more difficult to measure but there is little doubt that more is achieved by people working in groups as a team.

How does this relate to spirituality? Well, successful communities start by expecting differences and being willing to listen to one another. Their key values are caring for one another, respecting one another, listening to one another and remaining in dialogue. Resolving conflict is an aim of the spiritually minded.

There is much debate among politicians about whether there is such a thing as society and whether it is possible to build cohesive communities. My view is that community is at the centre of human existence. We do not live isolated lives, separate from everyone else; we live in groups of varying sizes which today tend to be more fluid that they were a few years ago. People form associations at work, in the rugby team, with other parents at their children's school, and so on, and these change through the passage of time. Communities also are much more dynamic than they used to be with people moving to follow jobs more regularly. However the neighbourhood and the wider community are still important parts of people's lives. People want to live in an area where community spirit is strong because they feel more secure and more fulfilled in such a community.

What sorts of things do people look for in community spirit? The keywords seem to be togetherness (people working together to solve problems); friendliness (having neighbours who are interested and interesting, have time for a chat and share a laugh); action for change (groups coming together to resolve an issue); shared purpose (people finding like-minded people to work together on common issues); social events (having the opportunity to meet together socially);

and inclusiveness (everyone feeling welcome). Notice that the word used is spirit; it shares a similar meaning to the way in which the word spirit is used in this book. It is about the higher and longer lasting values in life rather than material gain; it is intangible; it is mysterious in the way that it forms; it is about supporting and helping one another; it includes everyone; and it tries to improve life. The people who try to create a good community spirit are often called people of good will; this means that they look beyond their own short term interest to try to bring good things into existence for the whole community; they have a spiritual outlook on life.

Living in the world community

Many people would go along with me so far; they are happy with caring for friends, family, neighbours and their local community. But we need to go one step further and care for all others on the planet. We have learnt very clearly in recent years how interdependent the peoples of our world are. We talk about globalisation because we now know a lot more about the rest of the world and hear news from far away as quickly as news from close at hand. Trade increasingly takes place across the world. We share with our overseas brothers and sisters not only a common humanity but a common set of resources. Global warming has made this clear to us all. We now know that actions taken in one place have knock-on effects all over the world and vice versa. So it is in the interests of all to protect and build up people wherever they are.

Peace is a key element of living in the world community. All religions place a high value on peace but none more so than Buddhism which urges its followers to seek to be both peaceful and peace–makers. They are to work for personal peace (nirvana – peace, stability and freedom) and to bring peace (not as an end but as a step) into the world, which needs to be healed of its fragmentation. Buddhists believe that each look, smile, word and action can convey peace, and our survival as individuals and as a world depends on the practice of peace. Magnanimity is the Buddhist term given to the spirit growing larger (literally it means great soul), feeling inclusive and universal, reaching out to enfold others, erasing boundaries and enjoying one-ness; this is a desirable spiritual aim and a source of food for the soul, a paradox that our world can be both enormously large and yet intimately close. Equanimity is another term which is used to describe the calm, peaceful acceptance of the way things are in the present moment - accepting that what is, is ("if life hands you some lemons, then make lemonade"). It is about learning to smile and laugh at life, finding peace in the midst of pain, and realising that suffering is not overcome by avoiding it, but by facing it, going through it and moving on.

At the heart of the ways in which we are called to relate to one another spiritually there are three key words – loving, giving and serving – this chapter concludes by looking at each involves.

Loving

Let us try to picture a loving relationship. It begins with mutual respect and a desire to share. It looks for the best in the other. It forgives and re-builds. It broadens and facilitates growth. It puts the other first. It is self-renewing. It takes both the lover and the loved one outside of him or herself to a view of what the world should be like at its best. It sparks the imagination. It enriches the soul.

But to be loved, you need to love. How then do we love? First of all, by trying to understand other people and their situation, putting ourselves in their place. Shelley wrote[4]: "A man to be greatly good must imagine intensely ... he must

4   P. B. Shelley, "A Defence of Poetry", Harvard Classics, Vol 27

put himself in the place of another and many others ... the pains and pleasures of his species must become his own". Secondly, by taking action. Love is more than armchair sympathy. When Jesus taught about love, he did not finish his parables by saying "That is what love is like" or "That is who your neighbour is", but by telling people to "go and do likewise". Thirdly, by being prepared to suffer rather than to inflict suffering. The spiritual understanding of life demands that we should avoid taking action which is inconsistent with our overall purpose. The ends rarely justify the means. Love in action requires us not to meet evil with evil and not to take revenge. Our commitment is to a love which does not compromise. As soon as we compromise, we lose both the argument and our integrity.

Giving

At the heart of loving is giving. If we think of the world of nature or of art or of invention or of relationships, they are all sustained by giving. If the world did not give us food, or the artist did not give us beauty, or the inventor did not give us new methods or technology, or the loved one did not return our love, then everything that we trust in would fail and our world would collapse in a catastrophe of selfishness. At the heart of all human relationships is giving (of love, time, belief, trust, support, things) rather than receiving; after all, if there was no giving, there would be no receiving. Of course, receiving is also important, especially the way that we receive - with grace, thankfulness and appreciation. It is part of our soul's desire for relationship that we naturally give, but some of us have to learn how to give because perhaps we have not been given very much in our early experiences of life.

Giving is not particularly about material things; indeed the most important gifts that we can give are spiritual rather than material, such as honour, trust, belief, support, sympathy, and especially love. When I was a small boy, I had an autograph album into which friends and relatives wrote a message to me. My father wrote: "Smile for when you smile another smiles and soon there are miles of smiles – so smile"; it has stayed with me because it is true - try it! When you give away a smile, the person smiled at reciprocates and a good feeling is created. A song that my children learnt many years ago has the words "love is something, if you give it away, you end up having more"; again it is so true. Our soul, our essence, our genius tells us clearly that in our uniqueness we can give of ourselves to others and this is our purpose in life.

Giving is more than simply transferring goods from one person to another. It involves care and concern for the other and is a tangible way of showing our concern. I am told that Zulus (and perhaps other African tribes) show this in the way they receive; they do so with cupped hands in order to acknowledge the generosity of the giver (two hands) and to show respect and recognition that the spirit of compassion is alive in the one who is giving.

Caring is an aspect of giving. Caring is giving time and energy to others. Those who are in a position to care should find the time and energy to care for those who are in need. Often vulnerable people who are in need of care have been carers themselves in the past. Caring for others in the community has certain prerequisites: the carers need to be realistic about the situation as it really is, not what they would like it to be; caring involves working as a team, offering and receiving varied inputs; carers must offer kindness, patience, sensitivity, humility and willingness to learn; they must have a vision of how things might be and a commitment to the victory of the spirit.

Serving

We serve by doing things for other people; we are never more spiritual than when we are serving those in need. Serving involves us in abandoning self-interest or complacency and choosing to help. Serving has the same root as servant and the most fulfilling way of relating spiritually to other people is in the servant role – not as someone who is forced into service but as someone who chooses to give the other respect by serving. Such humility facilitates soul growth. Serving is important to community life. No progress is ever made unless there are people who are willing to serve others in making progress.

Sometimes we feel remote from other people because we feel that they are different, or threatening, or have let us down in some way or they have hurt us or offended us. We want to keep them at a distance. But it is crucial to the spirit that we should overcome prejudices, that we should never wish evil upon those whom we dislike and that we should always try to forgive. If we need forgiveness for our weakness and failures, we cannot possibly receive it unless we are forgiving of the weaknesses of our friends and our neighbours, wherever in the world they may be.

Serving involves giving without expecting any return. No one can be forced to accept our acts of love or service, nor should we expect them to. We must serve without counting the cost and without expecting any return. We are called upon to serve those in need not because we want thanks but because we are filled with the spirit of love.

Some points to consider

1. This chapter focuses on togetherness and relationship but some people find this difficult. Why do you think that this is the case?
2. What is your view of the breakdown of the traditional family in the west? Can you see advantages as well as disadvantages?
3. Do you live in a community with a good spirit?

How do you measure this? How can it be promoted?

4. What is your view of globalisation? Can you see its impacts on your daily life? Does it make you feel closer to those far away?

5. Can you produce a list of examples of people whose lives have been marked by their loving, giving and serving? What do you feel was their motivation?

7. Living ethically

One of the key ways of nurturing the soul is through ethical behaviour. This is much more than simply observing a minimum set of standards, which are usually negative in tone (i.e. don't do ...). It is a calling to a way of life or a philosophy of living in which we are concerned for the natural world and other human beings and seek to live with empathy and compassion. This is ethical living because it takes us out of our absorption with ourselves and leads us towards others. We act in this way because we believe that we are in this world together and that the good life comes from being creative together and taking our pleasures from one another. With such a view we find fulfilment in making a contribution, serving the needs of others and leaving self behind. We move on in our spiritual life through action and attitude and ethical living provides us with an opportunity rather than a demand. It is our soul which gives us our conscience (you might like to think of it as the soul making suggestions about becoming more soulful) and choosing to be faithful to our conscience makes us who we are.

Values

Living ethically is about putting into practice the values that are central to our world-view as spiritual people. Different individuals will have different priorities and we need to work out for ourselves what they are. One way of doing this is to write down the key values that govern our way of life which the last few chapters have been discussing. To prompt such an exercise below is a list which draws heavily on the inaugural address of Barack Obama in January 2009 and which can be used as a starting point for determining your values. He suggested that:

- all human beings are born equal and free and deserve the opportunity to find fulfilment in their lives;
- to achieve this they should have access to resources of food, shelter, medicine, education;
- those who are fit and well should take responsibility for the poor and vulnerable;
- we should deal with each other with integrity, honesty and tolerance and should seek justice for all;
- we should create conditions in which people can improve themselves by working hard, taking risks, exploring possibilities, pushing back boundaries;
- we have duties to our families, our neighbourhood, our country and our world – "duties to be seized in the knowledge that there is nothing more satisfying to the soul, more defining of character than giving ourselves to a difficult task"[5].

Living honestly and with integrity

The starting points for ethical living are honesty and integrity. There is nothing more important for us as humans than to live lives that have inner integrity; that is why we have been given a soul. Today we hear a lot about lives which are disintegrated being a source of mental, physical and emotional breakdown. If you live a false life, saying one thing and doing another, it catches up with you. If you live a cheating life, taking things that do not belong to you, sooner or later your conscience will challenge you and your world will come crashing down. Just as, if you eat inappropriate food or drink alcohol to excess, your body will fail to cope,

5   Barack Obama in his inaugural address as US President in January 2009

97

so, if you continue to behave in ways that are unhealthy, your emotional life or mental state will collapse around you.

If we are parents, we expect honesty from the children we love. If we find that a child is telling lies, we are horrified and hurt. Perhaps we have experienced the pain of discovering that someone, who has been speaking pleasantly to our faces, has been ridiculing or insulting us behind our backs. The deceit hurts as much as the actual offence. Spiritual living abhors hypocrisy, loathes falsehood and pretence. And there is nothing worse than pretending to prioritise the spiritual side of life if our lives show that we could not care less about other people.

If we are letting ourselves down, why does it take us so long to admit our failing? Why do we keep on pretending that there is nothing wrong with what we are doing? As soon as we make the first tentative move to desire honesty and integrity, we receive affirmation from those around us. Real and expensive sacrifices may need to be made but we will find that we are making them out of choice and without resentment. A saying attributed to Mahatma Gandhi is "Be the change you want to see". This is the ambition of all spiritual people.

If we listen to the voice of our soul and trust in its message of love, then we have an eternal truth within us that can sustain through any circumstances and give us the freedom and joy that we as humans all seek. To ignore this voice and become a self-seeking individualist is a denial of human spirituality; it leads to dishonesty and disintegration.

Living caringly

Living attentively (which was discussed in chapter 4) is simple to describe but seems to be difficult for people to achieve in the increasingly complex and pressurised world in which we live; it is about becoming completely alive and living each moment of each day deeply; and it is essential to soul growth. If we are talking to someone, it is about listening carefully to what they are saying; if we are watching people on a bus or at a party, it is about blessing them by being available should they be in need and thinking good things about them; if we are preparing a meal, it is about using our skills, the implements and the food carefully, to best effect; if we are out for a walk, it is about looking at the flowers, or the leaves, or the sky, or the birds and giving thanks; if we are using resources of the world, it is about being aware and careful not to waste them; and so on.

Once we learn to live attentively, we inevitably go on to live caringly because we see the essential importance and goodness of the people, the things and the world around us and we want to help preserve their goodness and contribute to building them up. It is similar to caring for a child. Unless we are mentally unbalanced, none of us would want to do harm to a child. We want to see him or her grow in grace and strength eventually developing into a young person full of hopes and dreams which he or she is free to fulfil. In other words, we nurture children because they are a wonderful, miraculous gift of the spirit of love. The same applies to the natural world in which we are placed, to the animals, the plants and the resources of the world. The same applies to man-made creations, machines, products, scientific discoveries or artwork. The same applies to other people, whether in our family, among our friends, in our neighbourhood or across the world. They are all given to us without our deserving them and they are there for us to care for.

Living in tune with the spirit of love shows itself most clearly in the way that we love other people. Let us consider in more depth the nature of love. Love is what we do when we put someone else ahead of ourselves, when we are prepared to make sacrifices for that person, when we seek the best for them at all times and in all ways. Love is about building someone up, not knocking them down. Love is about being patient when things seem difficult. Love is about forgiving when the other person does something which is hurtful. Love is about doing things for other people, not just thinking about doing them. Love is about making peace (not just wanting peace) when there is a breakdown. Love is about doing more than is expected. Love is about doing things that you don't like doing because they have to be done in caring for the other. Just think how wonderful the world would be for you if you loved all and received love from all.

Love is the highest form of relationship that you can give or receive. It is the ideal that all human beings seek. It is the urging of the spirit within us that we should desire to be loved and that we should give love. Sometimes people say to me 'how can you love someone that you do not like?' My reply is 'try it and see how good it feels for you and for them'. It is exactly this that the spirit of love urges us to do. Clearly our lives are finite and there is a limited number of people with whom we can truly have a relationship, but that number is much larger than most of us think and the joy that we can experience is much greater than we can imagine.

Of course, loving is risky, When you love, you become more vulnerable as you lower your defences and take a weaker position, promising to stand by and uphold the loved one in all circumstances. Some people find this very difficult to do and give up when things go wrong; sometimes they are turned off love forever because of a bad experience of being let down. But there is nothing more wonderful in life than experiencing or seeing someone loving to the ultimate, overcoming the feelings of vulnerability and giving themselves utterly to another or others. This is victorious living and it sets a vision before us of how life can be if we live in the freedom of the spirit of love.

Passion for justice

Recognising the power of the spirit in the world and allowing it to fill our souls has implications for the way we live our lives day to day. The spirit wants to change us from self-seeking individuals to people who are committed to one another, who trust other people and who seek the best for all. There is no clearer vision for a spiritual person than that of a world in which the weak are supported by the strong, the outcast are brought back into relationship with others, the poor are enriched, the lonely widows and orphans are embraced with love. Some would say that this is the type of world into which humans are born but which has been spoilt by the unwillingness or inability of some to see its beauty, freedom and joy.

All of the main religions have as a central tenet the relief and eradication of poverty and faith communities are at the forefront in working with the most disadvantaged in our world, often in very difficult situations. Spiritual people are compassionate towards those in need, provide practical help and campaign to challenge injustice. The spirit wants to see wrongs righted, unfairness corrected, suffering eradicated. However, because people see this not always happening in our earthly life, religions have tended to promise that the injustices will be put right in life beyond death. The difficulty with such a promise (ignoring the difficulty of proving it) is that it provides an excuse to do nothing about wrong and injustice during our earthly life. I believe in spiritual life beyond death as will be seen in a later chapter, but not in an arbitrary separation of the good from the bad which seems entirely inconsistent with the spirit of love. Rather I believe that what the spirit of love requires is people who are seized by a vision of freedom and justice and who use their earthly life helping to bring it about. Living in this way is living in the spirit.

Thus spirit-led people are filled with a passion for justice that will dominate their lives. They look for the right path; they challenge injustice; they care for those in need; they work to improve the lot of those who are disadvantaged. Charity is not enough, though it is important, because it is tinkering around the edges instead of tackling the root causes. A passion for justice involves challenging unacceptable systemic injustice and this affects every aspect of life. That is not to suggest that spiritual people do not make mistakes or do not from time to time let people down, but it does mean that, seen in the round, they will have lived a life which has tried to make things better for their fellow human beings.

Some of you may be feeling that the earlier section on caring was excessively naïve and optimistic because the world in which we live is not made up of people who are entirely lovable. Indeed it is clear that, whilst individuals are not inherently and irredeemably evil, nevertheless some events and situations, generated by human beings, are overwhelmingly evil. Examples would include the Nazi concentration camps, ethnic cleansing, indiscriminate bombing and excessive violence of any kind. The spiritual person's passion for justice will lead him or her to fight against such occurrences as far as possible by non-violent means but ultimately, if there is no alternative, by the use of force.

There is a limit to what we can do as individuals in our complex world, but we can give thanks for caring organisations that work across the world bringing relief to those who suffer from natural disasters, giving voice to the poorest and campaigning for political change in the richer nations so that poverty is tackled. Examples include organisations such as Christian Aid, Oxfam, Islamic Aid, CAFOD, Action Aid, UNICEF, and there are many others. Such organisations are a gift of the spirit to the world. They are trying to do the caring at a global level that individuals find so difficult to do. They provide us with the means to respond to our desire, inspired by the spirit of love within us, to love and serve the poorest people in the world. We can offer our time to such organisations. We can campaign through them, we can give and raise money through them and we can offer our talents in whatever way they best help the work of these organisations.

Working ethically

In the western world, the majority of people spend a large proportion of their life working to earn money to pay for what they consider to be the essentials of life. Indeed the right to have a job has been a dominant political issue for many years, with full employment being a target of most governments. As employment has increased it has not always brought with it greater choice of type of work. Jobs requiring a particular set of skills have a shorter time-span than in the early days of the industrial revolution. Skills that were in demand twenty or thirty years ago are no longer required as more and more tasks are automated. The number of jobs in agriculture is very small in most western countries, the number of jobs in industry is reducing at a rapid rate and the growing sector is that of so-called service industries.

As a result many people find themselves working in jobs that they do not like and wonder about the ethics of some business practices. In an ideal world, people would be able to choose their job to enable them to fulfil their spiritual inspiration. But the world is not ideal and sometimes jobs have to be done as a means to an end (i.e. earning money) rather than because they match one's true aspirations. For the spiritual person the first priority should be to try to find a job which enables them to fulfil their aspirations; if they are unable to do this, then to take on a job which gives them the means to do so. However, the spiritual person should always challenge unethical practices in any work situation. Honesty, integrity, caring and trust are ultimately of the highest importance.

Work should be an extension or reflection of yourself, giving you good feelings when you achieve something that makes you proud. This is far more important to the soul than the secondary rewards of money, prestige and the trappings of success. Climbing the ladder can easily be unsettling to the soul. Perhaps we ought to choose an employer by testing his values – the spirit of the workplace, how people are treated, feeling of community, people loving their work, ethical end-product and environment? Most work is ordinary, repetitious and boring unless we can approach it creatively (as described in the next chapter), trying always to do a good job, using our inventiveness to improve things and reflecting on methods and outcomes imaginatively. We all yearn for inspiring and exciting work but we have to realise that any work is full of the humdrum, frustrations, dead ends, mistakes and failures.

Work is more than making a living, it is participation in creative activity, and it is increasing the common good. It forms part of our human identity. It has significance and value in our lives. It should provide opportunities both to develop talents and to facilitate such rights as the right to a family, to private property, to become a stakeholder in society. Work helps people to develop attributes such as working together, perseverance, determination, openness, enthusiasm and commitment.

Work should never be oppressive or an affront to human dignity and anything that makes is so should be challenged by those with a spiritual understanding of life and eradicated. Any thing that involves too heavy a physical burden, too much mind-numbing labour, too long hours, too much risk to health must be fought against. The greater the burden, the more the need for rest and recuperation. Those who employ others should create conditions in which human dignity is protected, human rights are promoted, personal development is possible, and peace and security are maintained.

Handling our material possessions

We considered earlier how caring for the world in which we live is part of living ethically in the spirit. Many people say that part of the difficulty of living spiritually is the attractiveness of 'worldly pleasures'. By this they do not usually mean sexual or erotic pleasures which the words are often used to describe; they mean all of the material pleasures such as good food, fine wine, holidays in exotic places, fast cars, beautiful clothes, spa treatments, computer games, fine art, and so; the list is endless. However, these worldly pleasures are the privilege of a minority of people in the world. The vast majority live in abject poverty with inadequate food, shelter, clean water, medicines, jobs or education; and this majority are our neighbours whom we are called to love. We cannot simply enjoy our good fortune in being born at a time and in a part of the world which has relatively untold wealth and do nothing about those in great need. Each person has to decide how to deal with this ethical dilemma; at the very least, as much of our resources should be given to alleviating poverty as are given to personal enjoyment of 'worldly pleasures'.

Money is the means we have developed for dealing with community transactions and exchanges. We are paid for doing a job which has a value and we use our earnings to pay for services and products from others. These are the mechanics of most societies. There is, of course, a downside. People can become so obsessed with money that they are lured into greed. When greed, cheating or embezzlement take over, souls are damaged and money becomes an obstacle to spiritual living. Societies fall apart when corrupted in this way and the 2008 credit crunch in the west was a clear sign of these dangers.

It is important that we deal with money spiritually (i.e. think carefully about how we use the resources given to us). This involves recognising that true wealth is not to be found in money; that we must be prepared to pay for shared, community provision; that we should care for such community resources; that we should always be seeking to eradicate poverty; that we are stewards and not owners of the world which provides the majority of our 'wealth'; and that we should look after the world for those who follow.

We have been given a soul to help us to sort out the purpose of our lives, to give meaning and purpose to what we say and do. In order to understand what our soul is saying we need to listen to, and to reflect on, the spirit and then try to live in a way that fulfils the vision that we are given. The spirit tells us to live in a loving manner, caring about relationships before material possessions. We all know that acquiring things for their own sake offers no fulfilment beyond the immediate satisfaction of demonstrating wealth. And to do this while there are many millions of children around the world who are starving seems to me to be the essence of greed, dishonesty and selfishness. No one finds fulfilment in life through material possessions beyond the minimum required for health, safety and growth.

Developing a simpler life-style

Spiritual people have always been very aware of the dangers that material wealth presents to maintaining their awareness of the spirit and seeking to respond. They have developed techniques to keep their spiritual awareness sharp. Today we call the set of techniques asceticism. This word comes from the Greek word 'askesis', which means training (e.g. of athletes) through discipline. The great spiritual teachers have advocated fasting, solitude, self-denial, voluntary poverty, and staying the course as means to a greater good. Some ascetics have retreated to the desert or the monastery, either for life or for occasional refreshment, to exercise their discipline. Today such behaviour is often criticised as turning their backs on/escaping from the problems of real life. We need to find for ourselves an appropriate way of disciplining ourselves spiritually and meeting the challenges of saying no to certain ways of thinking, acting and being. It is not essential for spiritual people to withdraw but it is essential periodically to review our priorities in the use of our time, money and talents.

Time, money and talents are three of the things that we can give to others. For many people in the western world today, time is their most valuable commodity; pressures of various kinds (e.g. long working hours, travelling long distances, making unnecessarily large amounts of money) mean that time for others is at a premium and this can be a cause of marital breakdown and family tensions. As we respond to the promptings of the spirit, we may want to review our life-style and the way we use our time and ensure that more of it is given to caring for others in the family, among friends and in the world. The same thing applies to our money. There is no point in amassing wealth for the sake of it; if you become wealthy, use the wealth creatively for the benefit of others, including the poorest. With regard to talents, they are gifts given to us by the spirit and should be used in the service of the spirit; if there are things that we are good at doing, we should do them for others.

Some points to consider

1. Do you have a strong sense of conscience? Where do you think that it comes from?
2. What do you make of Barack Obama's list of values? Can you improve on it?
3. Is honesty important for you? Do you feel that

you are almost always honest or do you find the need to compromise? If so, why?

4. Do you feel a sense of obligation to care for other people? How far does this stretch? How do you put it into practice?

5. Do you have a passionate commitment to justice and eradication of poverty? If not, why not? If so, what do you feel that you can do to follow it up?

6. Do the paragraphs on work and money make sense for you or do you think that they are unrealistic? In either case, why?

7. Can you think of ways in which you could develop a simpler life-style?

8. Living creatively

The title of this book at one stage was to be "The spirit sets us free" and this is expressed no more strongly than in the way in which the spirit encourages individuals to be creative. The spirit is the creative and dynamic force at the root of existence; it is the power of love swooping over the universe, stimulating growth and newness, building up and enabling. The nature of love is creative in whatever sense we view it. Experienced in a relationship, it gives new life, transforming selfish thoughts into care for another. Experienced in the family, it nurtures and looks for the best for all members. Experienced in the workplace, it creates a pleasant and stimulating environment in which people are concerned for one another's well-being. Experienced by the individual in the world, it creates an active concern for the world, for people, for situations. All of these experiences are experiences of change and newness; instead of thinking only of oneself, and thereby sinking into self-preoccupation and ultimately despair, the spirit of love lifts us above our selfish interests to think primarily of the needs of others. In doing so, we look for the best for them and begin to create newness, growth and development. It is not possible for someone who is gripped by the spirit of love to seek to destroy or to hurt or to bring down; indeed it is a sure sign that the spirit is not working in us if we find ourselves engaged in activities that are destructive, hurtful and harmful.

Being creative takes various forms

The ways in which we can be creative are many and various. Some people think that creativity is the realm only of people who achieve things that are acknowledged to be exceptional, such as Mozart, or Leonardo, or Einstein, or Mother Teresa, or the Beatles, or Pele. But in all aspects of human life there are ordinary people doing things which exceptional people do. Most boys in the UK play football but only a very few have the talent, flair and commitment to become exceptional; this does not stop the remainder from playing and enjoying the game. Many young people learn to play a musical instrument but only a few become world-class musicians; this does not stop the remainder from enjoying music. Many adults find a job that they enjoy whilst never expecting to become the top of their profession. In all these examples, creativity is involved. Learning to do something new and improving our ability is creative, whether it is driving a car, repairing a bike, knitting a sweater, arranging a display of flowers, organising a party, arranging a holiday, visiting a friend in hospital, writing a letter in a political campaign, cooking a meal or engaging with a challenging television programme.

So what is creativity? It is acting in such a way that something is changed for the better. This involves being open to new ideas, learning from others and from mistakes, taking care in what we are doing, looking for an outcome that pleases those who will receive it, and giving our best to the activity. When we are doing these things, we are being creative. Of course, we cannot be creative all the time; our soul need periods of rest and relaxation, times when we are receiving rather than giving and times when we are learning. But when we are doing, we all have opportunities to be creative. Some people might argue that there are many jobs which involve a repetitive routine, requiring little thought or other input; this is the case but even in that type of job we can/need to be open to new ideas, learn from others and from mistakes, take care in what we are doing, look for an outcome that pleases those who will receive it, and give our best to the activity.

Let us look at a few examples of creative living.

Home-making

In the past home-making was seen as the role of women, but thankfully, as we have loosened the more rigid barriers in society, this is no longer the case. Now anyone can have the role of making their home a good place to be, whether for themselves, their family or their visitors. The role may be shared between partners or parents and children, or it may be the role of a person living alone.

The tasks involved in home-making are many and the responsibilities to others are high. Think, for example, of cooking, cleaning, washing, shopping, decorating, fitting out, making the home welcoming in appearance and in reality, creating an atmosphere where people, especially children, feel loved, respected and encouraged. These activities are very time-consuming and very important. Where they can they should be shared, even if one person takes the lead on particular aspects. And they all involve creativity: cooking is one of the most complex, involving creating savoury, healthy and attractive food for those who will share it; cleaning and washing can be seen as monotonous, but a creative approach looks for efficiency, effectiveness, order and loveliness; shopping involves creative decision-making, combining selection and fitness for purpose; decorating and fitting out require careful selection of colours and shapes that when implemented will please the eye; the latter will give a welcoming feel to the home but it needs to be enhanced by the creativity of making people personally welcome through care and hospitality; a home should be the place where the spirit of love is most felt so that children will grow up feeling cared-for and supported and adults will find a relaxed, non-threatening and constructive atmosphere.

Construction

The construction industry has been seen to be the preserve of men, but again it is common to see women more and more active in this type of work. Also the growth of 'do-it-yourself' stores to meet the desire of home-owners to develop their property means that many more people are engaged in aspects of construction that ever were.

Construction may seem like an obvious creative activity; it is concerned with constructing from scratch or renovating or improving an existing building. It is about making new, and it involves all the pointers which mark creativity: being open to new ideas, learning from others and from mistakes, taking care in what we are doing, looking for an outcome that pleases those who will receive it, and giving our best to the activity. So construction is undoubtedly creative and most of us engage in it in on one way or another. Whether the job is small (e.g. adding a porch to one's home) or large (e.g. converting a mill building into executive apartments) it needs to be well-planned and well-executed. We need to be careful about selecting the right materials and finding out about new techniques/technology. We need to find out how to do things that we have not done before and we need to learn from the mistakes we have made previously. We need to approach the job with care and patience to make sure that everything fits together in the right way. Throughout we need to bear in mind the desired outcome, so that it looks as good as we can achieve. And we need to do the best we can at all stages of the project so that the outcome is worthwhile.

The same kind of approach applies to gardening projects from making a window box to designing and implementing a new patio area. It applies to painting the outside of the house or changing a piece of guttering. It is true when working on the car or the mower or repairing the washing machine. If we want a good result, we need to tackle these projects creatively and we are all capable of doing so because the spirit of creativity has been implanted in our souls at birth.

Vocational work

Some jobs are described as vocational, by which people mean that the occupants have felt called to do the work. Teaching is one such job; others include nursing, social work, probation, medicine, local government, ministry, world development, and politics. In the past, a vocation was a job which paid less than many others but which carried respect in society and allowed people to fulfil an inner desire to serve people directly. Thus the caring professions were seen as vocations. Much of this no longer applies (e.g. doctors are among the highest paid, politicians are strongly tainted with self-interest and corruption, world development is trendy 'because it lets you see the world') but nonetheless people still feel called to particular types of work. What is the nature of this call? Can it still be fulfilled? In what ways are such jobs different from other jobs?

People who feel a call to do particular jobs may have many different reasons for feeling the call. It may arise from their family traditions, religious beliefs, desire for social standing, impression of the attractions of the job, careers advice, the interests of their friends, the subjects that they do well in at school or a role model in their family or friends. For some, there is a strong sense of call to do something to serve their fellow human beings. This is the spirit of love that is inspiring them to live out the promptings/inspirations that they experience. They feel a strong desire to do a worthwhile job (which they measure in terms of its direct influence of their fellow human beings) which will have long-term benefits. Teaching children, healing the sick, caring for the vulnerable, helping people to rebuild their lives, working with people who have nothing are all activities that meet these criteria. They are also a reflection of the criteria for creativity: openness, willingness to learn, care, looking for an outcome that pleases those who will receive it, and giving of our best.

Can such a call still be met by these types of job? Yes, to some extent. They still provide the opportunity to work closely with people and to serve their best interests but they no longer have the freedom and initiative-taking that used to be the mark of responsible professional jobs. Many of these jobs are now wrapped up in red-tape with many of the measures used in business brought in to assess achievement. Quantity rather than quality, outcomes rather than inputs and process, rules rather than imagination, and profit rather than people are key words today as politicians have brought business techniques into the public service. Some of this has been beneficial (e.g. more attention to value for money) and some of it has been brought on by the failings of previous job occupants (e.g. patient abuse). But the outcome is that vocational jobs have become more like so-called non-vocational jobs in banking, accounting, selling, manufacture, etc.

However, in the wealthy west the latter type of job has become more like the old idea of a vocational job. Now all jobs have a focus on people (especially, in the business jargon, on customers and clients), on teamwork as the means to achieve successful outcomes, and on job enrichment so that they are seen to be challenging, worthwhile and rewarding. The dominance of scientific management on treating people like cogs in a production machine has rapidly declined as technology has taken over the more routine tasks. The economies of many western countries have moved towards the service sector (as manufacturing has moved to cheaper, developing countries) where most jobs are about dealing with people (e.g. in fast food chains, in retail outlets, in call-centres). Employees are valued more for their interpersonal skills and entrepreneurship has become a watch-cry for many governments. Thus creativity is seen to be of greater importance and people are being given more chance to demonstrate the innate gifts of the spirit. Social background, family connections and educational qualifications are still important determinants of progress but are losing their hold.

Visual Art

We now have seen a model of creativity at work in home-making and in construction projects and have considered its role in vocational jobs. We will now turn to an activity that has been traditionally seen to fall more clearly in the creative area – visual art – and see what the differences are, if there are any.

Visual art is surface art that we enjoy through the use of our eyes and the way the brain processes the visual signals. It could be a painting, a tapestry, a relief carving in wood, a mosaic, a sculpture, a stained glass window, or anything else that we look at. To be called art it will normally have been produced simply to delight or disturb. Thus it would not normally include manufactured products, which are functional but a delight to see, such as a sports car or a yacht or a kettle, though some artists and art experts would disagree. A work of art would normally be considered to be artificial (i.e. not a product of nature), developed by a human being using skill and technique, which appeals to the viewer's ideas of beauty and gives him/her an insight into the world beyond his or her limited material existence. Not all people will necessarily appreciate the same piece of art and partly this is due to differing ideas of what is beautiful. A traditional definition of beauty would emphasise the interplay of harmony, unity/integrity and radiance; in other words the piece must be appropriate to its content/theme, created in a medium which communicates, have an inner consistency and make effective use of the constraints of space; one might add that it must seek after truth because truth (I.e. that which is internally consistent, genuine and honest) has a quality which lifts people out of themselves.

All good art has a spiritual dimension in that it gives delight, it provides insight and meaning, it inspires, it makes ultimate reality visible, and it draws out the capacity to understand the spirit at work. Good art comes from artists who feel passionately for their subject (i.e. are not disinterested) but seek honesty of interpretation, and who are willing to take risks whilst taking seriously the integrity of their artistic decisions.

In my experience artists have strong spiritual awareness. They are people on a journey, exploring their own sense of self and becoming spiritually more aware and open. Their spiritual life is an essential aid to their creativity. In a talk a practising sculptor expressed himself, as I remember, in these terms: "communicating in art is completely different from communicating in words", "my art is an icon or a window into the sacred by interpreting or taking a new view of what is seen", "art should offer hope and joy, should enrich and uplift". Making art is a creative act that draws its inspiration from the external world, incorporates images from memory, draws upon an active mind, and produces an image that points far beyond itself. Most artists are able to work with ideas and images that are not pre-constrained or pre-defined; they see depth in the observable world beyond what is immediately observable. Many people mean this when they speak of the sacred; artists help to reveal it.

Our response to works of art very much depends on our cultural context (e.g. memory, education, relationships, sensory stimuli, interests, needs and predisposition) and most of us need to be guided or taught how to look at art. Perhaps whether a work of art is good is ultimately subjective (i.e. does it touch a chord within you?) but we all have some kind of reaction to art. Our reaction may be mild or strong, positive or negative; we may be challenged, inspired, horrified, bored, delighted, baffled or disappointed.

I believe that the fact that we are all able to react in some way to works of visual art suggests that we are all capable of trying to produce such a work of art. Of course it would involve a lot of time learning the theory, techniques and styles of our chosen medium, studying work produced by exponents of our chosen genre, and developing our ideas/product. At the end of the process, we may find that not many people like what we have produced, perhaps because of poor technique but more probably because the style does not appeal to them. This does not mean that it is a poor piece of work; it simply means that there is insufficient consensus that it is exceptional. We are all capable of producing works of art, given the desire, the time and the training, because the spirit of creativity is in our souls.

Music making

The same applies to music making, traditionally seen as one of the key creative activities which are the preserve of the few. There is no doubt that some people are born with a natural affinity for music and music making; we can think of Mozart or Menuhin or McCartney whose gifts were so strong that they have given the world a huge amount of pleasure from their innate feel for melody and rhythm, enhanced by study of technique, method and the works of their forerunners. They were open to new ideas, they learnt from others and from mistakes, they took care in what they were doing, they looked for outcomes that pleased those who received them, and they gave their best to the activity.

We all take pleasure from music in one form or another. All over the world, music plays an important part in people's lives. For some it is in the form of CDs and downloaded files of recorded music to be listened to at will; for others it is the background to life in the supermarket or on the television; for others it is in the way their emotions are swayed by a soundtrack or at a concert; for others it is the pleasure of playing on their own or as part of a group. Even in societies that do not have the wealth or the complex technology of the west, music, rhythm and dance are fundamental to people's lives. We are all blessed with that spirit which enables us to recognise, to respond to, to be moved by and to enjoy music. This convinces me that, with time and effort, we can all make music. Children who learn a musical instrument at school, even though they may not follow it up later in life, find satisfaction, if they practice sufficiently, from what they can produce and never lose the feel for music that they have been given.

Even later in life, if we have the time, we can start to learn a musical instrument and can get great pleasure from playing it. It is not easy but most of the things that give lasting pleasure to human beings are not easy; part of the pleasure is the sense of achievement in overcoming the difficulties. A concert pianist of my acquaintance took up playing in his forties and became well known, playing concerts in several parts of the world.

Watching television and using the Internet

You may be wondering at this stage why there has been such an emphasis in this chapter on work when increasingly people have more time on their hands for leisure. So let us turn to two of the ways in which people spend their leisure time in the wealthy west – watching television and using the internet. How can we be spiritual in these activities?

The answer is that, as with most areas of life, our choices determine the extent to which we foster or undermine our spirituality and creativity. Television and the internet are both media for making available information and entertainment to people. They do so increasingly by pushing as much material as they can create, regardless of quality or desirability, on to the airwaves and leaving it to individuals to pull on to their television or computer the information or entertainment that they wish to select. The result of this is that there is a very large amount of material available which is of very poor quality, especially if judged against spiritual criteria such as: does it promote loving, caring relationships; does it build people up or bring them down, does it encourage creativity, does it foster harmony, peace, freedom and forgiveness? If it does not do these things, then its value has to be questioned.

Spiritual use of the internet and television requires us to be highly selective. It does not expect us to carry on watching simply to have something on view. It is very careful about what children are able to see. It sets a maximum time for use so that other abilities than watching continue to be stimulated. It chooses programmes and sites which are worthwhile and ignores the remainder. You have been given a soul that will help you to discern what is good. Think hard about the kind of world that you would like for your children and any website or television programme that does not help to create such a world should be dismissed. And when you find programmes and sites which are beneficial point them out to others and recommend them.

One of the great things about increased leisure, of course, is that people have more time to enjoy the world and all that it offers. Keeping fit by walking, swimming, playing sports, and eating more carefully will give you a better feeling about life. Many people are spending less time with the computer and television so that they can enjoy the wonders of nature, animals and other human beings. This is a good sign.

Some points to consider

1. What does the word creativity mean to you? How do you express it in your life?
2. Why do some people think of home-making as drudgery?
3. Why do people get satisfaction from making things?
4. If you have a job, what are your feelings about it? Why do you feel that way?
5. Can you define beauty in visual art or music`? What is it that makes something beautiful for you but not necessarily for others?
6. Does the final paragraph on television and the internet ring true to you? Why? How do you put into practice the idea of being selective?

9. Living prophetically

What is meant by 'living prophetically'? Spiritual people have a vision of the world as it was meant to be and could be if all people recognised and embraced the spirit. 'Living prophetically' involves telling others about this vision and its implications for the way in which we live our lives in order to give them the possibility of embracing the spirit in their lives. Sometimes this is about speaking from the heart about what we have experienced, sometimes it is about speaking the truth and calling people to a better way of living, and sometimes it is about engaging in argument to present a modern view of spiritual living.

Speaking about spirituality

The first prophetic task is, on the face of it, simple. It is to talk to others about one's experience of the spirit. We may want to talk about the song of the birds at dawn or the beauty of the flowers in spring, or the awesome image of the sun setting at the end of a lovely day. We may want to talk about the spiritual message for us of a particular painting, or film or piece of music. We may want to describe to someone our joy at a spiritual act of loving, comforting, healing, praising or blessing, carried out by others or by ourselves. We may want to talk about a job well done, a person finding fulfilment, an act of sacrifice, or an example of effective teamwork. Whatever it is that we want to describe to people should be expressed in the context of the spirit at work in people bringing out the best in them, personally, professionally, artistically, and in relationships. We see instances of eternity in these occurrences; not everyone does and our prophetic job is to give them insight into our way of seeing things.

We may also want to decry examples of brutality, greed and selfishness that we see around us or read about in the papers or see on the television. We should never be only negative but always offer ideas about a better way of seeing and living. There is no point in simply criticising because those listening may have no idea that there are other possibilities; our job is to present the positive alternative.

This chapter began by saying that this seems to be a simple task but it isn't. Presenting a spiritual vision needs gentleness and occasions don't always lend themselves to gentleness; it needs time and people seem to be in a perpetual rush; it needs some knowledge of the person's situation and we do not always have that knowledge. Nonetheless we should try whenever we can to give people a vision of what is possible for them.

At the end of the day, what matters most is not what we say but how we live. People are attracted to particular ways of living and finding fulfilment through seeing the way others with a similar outlook live their lives. People see the way we behave and think and act and respond when they see integrity and wholesomeness. This is the best way of prophesying.

Speaking about justice

We have considered in the chapter on ethics how the spiritual understanding of life is passionate about justice. In this chapter we need to reflect on the fact that justice is not the same as private charity. Justice is about trying to change the status quo in all situations where people are diminished or disempowered as a result of poverty or war or racism or sexism or wasteful lifestyles. In other words it is about trying to change systems which perpetuate unfairness and inequality; it is about campaigning for all people to be valued as human beings. There is a danger that we may be ethically upright in our private lives (compassionate, honest, caring, generous) but unwittingly give support to systems which are the opposite perhaps through our job or our political affiliation or our investments or our lifestyle. We may fail to realise that a system which is comfortable for us may be hurtful to others.

Thus the spirit encourages thoughtful people to examine all systems on the criteria of whether they unfairly penalise others and, where they are found to do so, to challenge them, to refuse to participate in them and to seek to change them. The spirit teaches us that all human beings are equally valuable and should be treated with respect. They are entitled to equal access to opportunity and resources and any right of private ownership or wealth accumulation should always take this into account. Social justice demands that we come to the aid of those in need and living prophetically means that we must proclaim this truth even if it is unpalatable in a given political and cultural climate. The condemnation of injustice, unfairness and excess is common to all religions and is an absolute requirement of the spiritual life.

Defending pluralism

We live in an age, especially in the west, where many ideas and solutions are on offer to people seeking the best way of living. People are no longer prepared to do or believe what they are told; the scientific age has encouraged them to question everything and to regard themselves as having the right to choose. So they have been encouraged to believe in such things as unashamed greed, winning the lottery, sport, sex, alcohol and drugs, violence, celebrity, glamour, physical fitness, and so on, as ways to find happiness and contentment. Most of these are prompted by commercial pressures in the media and pander to people's self-image in order to get them to make a purchase. They have nothing to do with ultimate happiness, peace and fulfilment.

Religions of many types and origins are also on offer, which do try to address ultimate values. Unfortunately, they have become increasingly scorned because they are seen to be authoritarian, to have been at the heart of war, cruelty and violence over the centuries, to be populated by hypocrites, with their followers either not understanding or not following their key teachings. Elements from within the religions are now being packaged as pick and mix spiritual offerings, without the dogma and rules of the religion from which they come.

We live in the west in an age of people making their own choices rather than being told what to do and what to believe. There are many virtues in this but it is also a source of great confusion. People want to exercise their choice based on experience but there is too much choice and not enough time. The old certainties have gone and people feel lost and easily misled. However, it is not possible to go back to a time of people being told what to do, nor would it be desirable to do so.

Thus we need to recognise that we live in a pluralistic age, in which no one idea or paradigm is seen to hold everlasting truth or a complete explanation of life on earth. This includes the great religious paradigms as well as the scientific and rationalist paradigms. All are relative and have their own origins and story (world-view) which makes them no more absolutely correct than any other. We should no longer expect people to believe because they are told; they have to find out for themselves.

This is why speaking about spirituality is important. In a pluralist age, when many competing ways of looking at life are on offer, people need to be sensitised to their spiritual origins and destiny. They need to have the spiritual side of life drawn to their attention. They need to be shown that there is an eternal dimension to life which gives meaning and purpose. At the beginning of this book we noted that all people are born with the spirit inside them; so why does it need to be pointed out to them? The reasons are that: most people in the west are no longer exposed to the teachings of any religion, which for all their faults may have led them to consider the spiritual dimension of life; at the same time people are bombarded by the media with short-term routes to short-term happiness and have in many cases lost the ability to differentiate the short-term (stimulated by commercial pressures) from the long-term truths which lie within them; and this is happening at a time when they want to experience things before they will put any trust in them.

Proclaiming the truth

So living prophetically is about proclaiming the truth – in two ways: firstly by reminding people of the eternal truth which lies within their soul, the spirit of truth, which enables them to discover eternal fulfilment; and secondly by telling them the truth about life.

Much of what appears in the media (magazines, newspapers, television, radio, the internet) is not true in the ultimate sense and does not seek to be; it does not measure itself against spiritual values and does not on the whole seek to promote them. The provision of information and entertainment today is almost without exception a commercial venture; it is not concerned with absolute truth but with 'relative' truth. In other words the pursuit of truth (i.e. accurate and thorough reporting) is tempered by questions such as how much does it cost, how much value will it add, how entertaining is it, what is the least we can get away with, and what does the owner want us to say. Thus we find some newspapers giving opinions rather than accurately reported news because opinions are cheap to acquire whereas accurate news is costly. We find some television channels offering artificially created programmes as if they are reflections of real life. We find some magazines devoted to finding and/or creating celebrities who can be persuaded to do outrageous things that can be embroidered upon in order to titillate their readers. We find some radio programmes which are simply recorded music (very cheap to broadcast) or talk shows on which people usually with little knowledge of a topic demonstrate their ignorance in public (sometimes even cheaper) or phone-in quiz shows with prizes in which the outcomes have in some cases been shown to be rigged. We find on the internet a plethora of websites which people construct to publicise themselves and which may have no resemblance to truth; there are benefits from the internet in that it allows people to find out facts very quickly if they are careful but sadly these are outweighed by the effects of salacious sites which are selling drugs, sex, violence and pornography and which attract the highest traffic.

People in the west are in danger of losing their way by allowing their lives to be dominated by a commercial, materialist style of living, failing to recognise that there is far more to human life than short-term, often unreal, pleasures of immediate gratification. The spiritual way is being crowded out by the market-place and huge numbers of people in the west are being deceived in the name of profit. The spiritual way needs to be manifested more clearly to people as an alternative to the tawdry, short-term experiences to which people feel they are called.

All of us want to live in a world or a culture that is authentic – this is what integrity is all about. What does authenticity mean? It means being surrounded by things that are important for us, that are real and engaging, that are true to themselves, and are positive and caring. When we look at television or films or books or newspapers we do not want to find the banal, the crude, the worthless. We don't want a culture of emptiness or mindlessness. We do not want to see people laughing at the humiliation of others. We do not want parades of materialism. We do not want to watch self-centred celebrities or foul-mouthed entertainers. We do not want what is most crass or stupid paraded before us as if it is what is best about modern living.

We want a world that is thoughtful and intelligent, that takes people seriously, that is concerned for the truth, that seeks to build up rather than to mock and destroy. We want to see a return to honesty and reliability and loyalty and consideration for others – the things that are essential for human beings to grow and flourish and for communities to be good place to belong to. We want to be reminded that we are a family of human beings which grows and prospers through caring and trust.

Authenticity also involves being allowed to question, to learn, to understand and to develop one's own ideas and beliefs. This involves challenging ideas and dogma that is not consistent with our own spiritual journey. The journey is not about being told but about discovering by being open to new ideas and to other people's experiences and values. It is about developing and expressing our own spirituality. This requires a spiritual community which is more questioning and less certain, which creates opportunities for people to talk things through, work out their own interpretations, confront puzzling ideas and meditate on their own experiences.

So where is truth to be found today? It is to be found in ordinary people going about their daily lives, caring for one another, living consistently, being honest with one another, bringing up their children not to tell lies and seeking the good things in life. It is to be found among caring individuals often in the caring professions, such as teachers, nurses, doctors, social workers and ministers. It is to be found among those who give their time to people and causes without seeking any financial reward.

Spiritual politics

Some people are strongly opposed to the intermingling of politics and religion but this position seems to be strange since all human beings should be concerned for the development of their community and society and we have found political systems the best way of dealing with such matters. Spiritual living is inevitably political because it seeks change in society; it should be interested not in keeping out of the 'dirty' political process but in persuading people that change can be brought about in ethical and spiritual ways. Spiritual people should make moral claims and challenges and should seek to overcome systemic injustice. Politics is about changes in peoples' hearts and minds; it is about sacrifice on behalf of the next generation; it is about we rather than I. Having said all of that, the spiritual person (unlike some self-seeking politicians) must always keep things in proportion, listen to the other viewpoint, be willing to bend and remain open to new ideas, whilst not deserting key principles.

Truth is more likely to be found where people act spiritually. Where material gain is involved, there is a danger that the truth may be distorted. In the past there was a general consensus that honesty mattered, that people should help one another, that cohesion in society was worth protecting, that service to others was very important and that some things have a value that cannot be measured in monetary terms. Now most things have to be measured financially; targets dominate the way people operate; success is measured in terms of wealth; and intrinsic worth has been replaced by extrinsic, measurable value. Many teachers feel that they are judged less for the atmosphere they create in the classroom than for their assessment results; some doctors complain that they are rewarded not for a caring approach but for the number of patients handled; artists are concerned that works of art are assessed for commercial value rather than artistic merit. We have been led by some politicians to believe that all that matters is greed and selfishness; the more selfish and greedy we all are, so the line goes, the better off we will become. These same politicians are unwilling to believe that people are more interested in caring than slaving for money; are reluctant to offend commercial interests in the media; and are unable to stand up for what is right in case it challenges the greed and selfishness manifesto. So we find ordinary people having to give more money to good causes (e.g. to tackle the after-effects of the Tsunami in South East Asia in 2005 or the floods in Bangladesh in 2007) than the government does!

The argument that the only thing that stimulates human beings into action is money is not a new one but it has gained popularity among politicians of most hues in the past 30 years. Nothing, in my view, could be falser. Almost all of the significant, lasting and life-changing achievements of human beings over the centuries came without financial incentives. They came from discoveries/experiments made by people who were motivated by their love of humanity or their innate inquisitiveness or their individual genius. People are motivated by the spirit, not by the acquisition of wealth. However, these politicians seem to believe that people are only interested in acquiring more goods, and that they cannot challenge the power of big businesses whose interest is in seeing growth in their own wealth.

Spiritual people are called to make clear to politicians that selfishness and greed are not acceptable and that truth, honesty, decency and caring matter far more.

Living intelligently and with discernment

The saddest feature of our current western situation is that we live in an age when people are better educated and have access to more information than ever before but so many seem to be incapable of living intelligently and with discernment in living their daily lives. The western world has become dominated by the commercial imperative which reduces everything to profit levels.

The greatest things that the spirit gives to all of us are knowledge, freedom and love – the abilities to think, to decide for ourselves and to care for other people. God wants us to use the gifts that he gives us at birth in order to fulfil our birthright as human beings.

First of all, the spirit gives us intelligence (to a much greater degree than any animal) so that we can enjoy and develop the world into which we have been placed. Over the years human beings have used this ability with great success and made huge progress, but in recent years we have lost respect for the world which we have on trust and have started to destroy it. Certainly the scale of exploitation of our planet has accelerated with little thought being given to the consequences. There are signs that our intelligence has made us too big for our boots so that we believe that we can do anything. This will only lead to disaster. We need to respect our given intelligence and use it wisely within the parameters of preserving the world in a good state for its future inhabitants. We also need as individuals to use our intelligence to discern what is good for us and for all people, and we have an obligation to the spirit to use it all the time.

Secondly, the spirit gives us freedom to make decisions. We are not robots compelled to act in particular ways. We are free to choose and we are given intelligence to weigh up alternatives in order to find the better way and the gift of love to provide us with the criteria which help us to decide. Freedom is what distinguishes us from animals and is the source of our creativity and uniqueness. We are not created to be unthinking slaves of a master (whether human or ideological); we are created as thinking humans free to gather evidence, to judge and to commit. There is no excuse for us to sit back and accept the propaganda which is thrust before us everyday; we are obliged to use our intelligence and freedom to think things through and to make appropriate choices. We are not bound to a selfish and greedy lifestyle.

Thirdly, the spirit gives us the gift of love, the ability to relate to others wherever and whoever they are. The spirit tells us that we have not been placed in the world for our own selfish good at the expense of everyone else who is sharing the planet with us during our earthly life. We have been placed here with all other human beings so that we can collectively care for the world, develop and improve it for those who follow. If everyone were here simply for themselves, the world would not only be a miserable place to live in but it would fall apart. In practice, people have loved one another and the world sufficiently for it to survive and flourish. When we look around and see the effects of violence, warfare and greed on people, none of us want it. That is because the natural state of humans, filled with the spirit, is to love; it is only when individuals fail to follow the spirit's call that they create pain and destruction. The spirit wants us to use our knowledge and freedom in defence of and for the propagation of love. So when we are faced with a choice, the spirit wants us to choose the loving way.

Valuing the eternal

We have come full circle in our discussion of living prophetically. It started by saying that we need to speak out about the spirit in our lives but acknowledged the difficulty of doing so. It, therefore, emphasised the importance of the way we live in influencing other people. We should live lives that place value on the eternal and not the immediate and transient. What does this mean?

If we value the eternal, we look at things with the eyes of the spirit using our intelligence, freedom and love and try to make decisions and take actions that are consistent. If we value the immediate and transient, we look no further than the next point of gratification with no thought for those around us whom we claim to love, nor for ourselves, physically and mentally. The following are some examples.

You may be tempted to spend your last banknote on a lottery ticket. You know that it would help with the family groceries or buy a birthday gift for a nephew or feed a starving person. You hope that you will win a prize but know that it is very unlikely (the odds against are too high) but you spend it anyway for the thrill of buying a chance. The purchase of the ticket has set aside your intelligence and the spirit of love.

You meet a handsome man or woman at a party, talk to him or her and discover that s/he is married with two children. S/he is lively and amusing and you feel sexual attraction. S/he has too much to drink and you find it easy to seduce him or her. The short-term desire for sexual pleasure shows lack of intelligence and no concern for their partner and children.

Your friends are into drugs. So far you have resisted partly because of the cost, partly because you are afraid of the after-effects and partly because you do not want to encourage others. One friend tries to persuade you by threatening to end the friendship if you don't join the group in partaking. This time you make a firm decision to have nothing to do with drugs. You have used your intelligence, freedom and concern for others to reject the short-term in favour of the eternal.

Your job is being made redundant. You start applying for other jobs, but nothing comes along until one day you are asked by an acquaintance if you would like a job at a warehouse. You go along to find out what is involved and you are told that no interview is necessary and you will be taken on immediately provided that you turn a blind eye to some illegal shipping. Although you need the money and your wife is expecting your first child, you immediately refuse the job, setting aside the short-term benefits in favour of honesty.

Your child is being bullied at school. You know who is doing it and you think about meeting him on the way home and confronting him. But you realise that this would give a bad example to your child and that taking the law into your own hands is always only short-term in its effect. You decide not to do it and instead go into school to talk to the teacher. You are intelligently and caringly placing the long-term solution ahead of the short-term gain.

The last three of these examples have a negative dimension (i.e. you are rejecting the short-term solution in favour of the long-term eternal). A more positive way of looking at valuing the eternal is looking for opportunities to encourage and develop others. Here you are not rejecting a particular path but choosing to value the eternal at all times. So in any situation you look for whatever is best for others (e.g. praising and commending achievement, helping a disabled person without patronising them, showing a youngster how to do something worthwhile, helping in a youth group, being chair of a PTA, working for a development charity, giving money regularly to a good cause). Valuing the eternal is allowing the spiritual to win when faced with ethical choices; it makes sense and it is always victorious. People see the spirit at work and are influenced.

Some points to consider

1. Do you think that people who have a spiritual understanding of life should try to convince others to have the same? Why?
2. In what ways do you consider that our western society has become more pluralist? Do you think that this is a good or a bad thing?
3. Is truth important to you? How do you measure it?
4. Are you involved in politics? If not, can you pinpoint why not and what would need to change for you to get involved?
5. Do you feel that you live intelligently and with discernment? If not, why not? If yes, how does it show itself in the way that you live?
6. Can you think of examples of times when you have used eternal values in deciding how to deal with a situation?

10. Living reflectively through prayer

One of the most important ways for the soul to be enriched is through reflection and the commonest way in which this is done is through prayer. Prayer is the name given to the way in which religious people relate to or communicate with the spirit, spending time learning and sharing. It is a bit like having regular conversations in which we talk and listen and come close to the spirit in our lives. Giving thanks, saying sorry, seeking further insights, expressing concern for others are all legitimate elements of such communication and help us to come closer to the spirit and to bring spiritual values into our lives, our homes, our families, our workplaces, our communities and the world around us. It is our way of becoming more sensitive to the spirit.

What is prayer?

Prayer is a fundamental action of spiritual people, through which they demonstrate their trust and belief in the power of the spirit and their connectedness to it. Prayer can be offered individually or in the company of like-minded people. It is about purposefully taking time out to acknowledge the transcendent in the midst of our everyday lives. It is about reflecting regularly on our experiences, trying to understand them in the light of our spirituality, and seeking to know how to respond. Some religions encourage the faithful to pray without ceasing - at all times and in all places – as they encounter the many situations that they face day-by-day. Others identify the need to set aside particular times of the day and for the inclusion of certain elements in prayer, for example, praise, confession, thanksgiving, offering, asking for help and blessing for ourselves or those in need, and listening for direction and purpose.

Whilst we may feel that our prayers will always be imperfect, because they are imbued with our human weakness, part of the discipline of living spiritually (i.e. remaining grounded in the spirit of love and life and opening oneself up to the spirit in others) is reflection through prayer. Prayer helps us to recognise our failings (whilst being made aware of loving support), to struggle with the demands on us (whilst receiving insights), to express our concerns for others (whilst retaining hope) and to find the peace that comes from spiritual blessing.

Different religions and denominations have different ways of praying but they all have the same two elements: first, reflecting through the spirit of love on things that have happened to us, things that are happening around us in our neighbourhood and in our world, and things that are particularly of concern; second, asking for our own actions and those of others to be brought into alignment with the spirit of love.

The various ways of praying include: using a liturgy (in which appropriate words have been written in advance to help in prayer); using the sacred scriptures of the religion; quiet contemplation from time to time each day when we see something to give thanks for or to seek change in; meditating on a poem or text or film or painting (any form of communication which provokes us to reflect); reciting and repeating a set of words or mantra; and using aids to prayer such as bells, beads and incense. Prayer can take place at any time and anywhere, but most religions expect adherents not only to pray in private but also to gather for communal prayers.

It is important not to think of reflection through prayer as simply an intellectual exercise in which the only faculty used is the mind. Prayer involves turning the body, the mind and the heart towards the spirit, allowing the soul to interact with the spirit. Sometimes the body needs to be at rest, able to be quiet and to focus; at other times prayer is noisy and celebratory, particularly with others and at specific times, perhaps involving hymns, psalms and responses. The mind needs to be focused, sometimes taking the lead by identifying subjects for prayer, sometimes waiting quietly for and receptive to the spirit's word; the mind concentrates on making sense of what is being said. The heart needs to bring forward the feelings that are to be voiced in prayer and to make a commitment to the consequences that emerge, whether further reflection, joyful celebration, going to visit someone in need, writing a letter or going to hear a speaker. Having a personal encounter with the spirit in prayer involves love, and love comes from the whole being i.e. from the soul, where the spirit is growing. When we pray with our soul, the spirit is praying in us.

An important part of prayer is receiving or listening. Messages can come in many different forms – through nature (a place, the colour of flowers, snow, water), through words (a book, a song, a discussion, a poem), through people (their actions, their facial expressions, their values), through art (music, painting, architecture, sculpture).

How do we think about the spirit?

The way we think of the spirit has a huge influence on the way in which we pray. Traditional ideas of gods as intervening and external powers in the universe have led to particular types of prayer. For example, those who think that their god is an all-powerful force capable of independently changing events and actions tend to pray either to appease this god or to ask for things that they want that they think their god can deliver. Those who think of their god as a powerful friend, working on the side of believers, tend to ask for the things that they think they deserve. Those who see gods as arbitrary and remote powers who cannot be easily influenced tend to perform perfunctory prayers to try not to be disturbed. Those who think that their god is weak and open to persuasion use their prayers to tell him/her of the things that they will do in return for favours. Those who see their god as rewarding people who pray will pray as often and for as long as they can. Those who see their gods as unable to see clearly that they are among the most loyal spend their prayers trying to convince them of their misconception. Most of these ways of praying are based on a false understanding of the nature of the spirit.

If, instead, we see the spirit as a force of creative love, alive within us and in our world, accepting us as we are and actively loving us into goodness, then our approach to prayer is completely different. It involves us in spending time listening to that force within us as it tries to show us how to live our lives. It encourages us to be open to the prompting from within us and from the world outside as we see evidence of the spirit at work in the world. It leads us to ask that we may be filled at all times with that power of love, surrendering our souls to the spirit that we can trust completely. It enables us to recognise and give thanks for the faithfulness of the spirit who never changes and always supports and encourages us. It prompts us to look for unexpected ways of finding this love and accepting the challenge that this implies. It expects us to put trust and faith in the spirit who is infinitely patient in waiting for us. It gives us opportunities to experience the freedom which comes from trusting and being open to the spirit. Our prayers may still involve praising, thanking, asking, giving and blessing but our prayers are much more meaningful if we have this understanding of the spirit at work within us and in the world.

Asking prayers

To illustrate the difference in approach that is involved in the different ways of thinking about the spirit, we can perhaps consider the use of asking prayers, called intercession when the prayer is for other people and petition when it is for ourselves. Intercessory prayer is natural to those who believe in a spirit of love in order to express their compassion and anxieties. Such prayers are grounded in trust and we pray for others because we love them, we want to express our concerns for them, and we want to affirm that we are ready if need be to be used to bring help and support to them. This is part of that belonging to one another, which is an essential component of spiritual living. Typically such prayer moves outward from the self; self→ family → community → world.

If we conceive of the spirit to whom we pray as an external, intervening force, our prayers will tend to concentrate on some of the following:

- informing the god about the situation or about our concern for it on the grounds that he/she needs to be told;
- persuading the god to act or intervene in a set of circumstances in order to alter them, thereby removing from us our freedom of thought and action;
- asking the god, who is in place A to go to place B, where he is needed, thereby denying that he/she is present with us all of the time;
- expecting an immediate answer to prayer because we only see answers in terms of fulfilment of our own wishes;
- confining our prayers for others to times of crisis (e.g. asking for water only at a time of drought, or praying for war to be ended only at a time of war).

If, however, we conceive of the spirit as operating within us in our soul in the core of our being, our prayers will be quite different:

- We will ask for things that are consistent with our experience of the spirit;
- We will pray for what is best (most worth having) for people e.g. being filled with the fullness of the spirit, being healed, receiving grace and mercy and strength;
- We will ask to be part of the spirit's purpose and channels through which love can act;
- We will spend time quietly seeking the best way forward;
- We will recognise that in praying for another we become inextricably bound up with that other; a prayer that is simply a request, without self-offering, is not a prayer in the spirit.

Forms of talking to the spirit

People have always found talking or telling much easier than listening and reflecting. The western religious liturgies fall mainly into this first category. They consist of written prayers which people can read or recite together or in the privacy of their home. They usually address the areas mentioned earlier:

- Adoration and praise of God
- Confession of our failure to live out the standards to which we lay claim (often accompanied by an assurance of forgiveness pronounced by a priest)
- Thanksgiving and offering
- Supplication or petition (asking for things for ourselves)
- Intercession (asking for things for others)

- Dedication/commitment to living life God's way.

These are all concerned with telling God. They often draw on spiritual treasures in scripture or written by faithful people; sometimes they are personally composed for a specific occasion. But their role is to facilitate congregational participation, sometimes through spoken responses, in worship.

Instead of liturgical prayers such elements of prayer may be delivered extempore or spontaneously, though those who advocate liturgical forms would criticise spontaneous prayers as tending to be exclusive and repetitive.

Forms of listening to the spirit

Ways of encouraging people to listen and reflect on what they have learnt were slower to develop, partly because the ordinary people did not have the means to acquire or use written or visual aids. In the early religions the reading of scriptures, use of images and ritual practices were the main ways in which people were directed to reflect on what God was saying to them. There were opportunities for more open or invitational prayer when other members of the gathered community might volunteer ideas, experiences (e.g. testimonies) and concerns for others, but these were less frequent. Silent prayer in corporate worship was not common, but individuals were encouraged to use silence and solitude to listen to God's promptings in the privacy of their homes. In the eastern religions, however, there has always been a stronger emphasis on reflection, meditation and contemplation.

Meditation was the name given to reflective prayer which was intended to deepen the participant's love of neighbour. It tended to be based on ancient scriptures which were recited by the monks (e.g. among the Jews (*Haga*) and

Muslims (*Dhikr*)). Lay people were encouraged to learn key parts of the scriptures by heart. In Christianity the Mass was a focus for meditative devotion in the high middle ages (when it was watched but not consumed), with the priest's dramatic vestments highlighting the passion story. In other religions, images of the gods and use of ritual were of crucial importance in helping the faithful to gain an understanding of the faith.

We can perhaps draw two illustrative examples of meditative prayer from the Christian past. One is called *Lectio Divina;* Saint Benedict in the 6th century in forming the Benedictine order of monks encouraged them to devote about four hours of each day to *lectio divina*, reading Biblical passages to a programme over a fixed period that covered the whole Bible, with *meditatio* or 'rumination' on the texts, and prayer in private; the early monks were rooted in an oral culture; many were not literate; so they learned texts by heart in the fullest sense. The other is the *Jesus Prayer* which has a long tradition within the Orthodox Church as an oral prayer said repeatedly aloud until it becomes inward, without movement of the lips or tongue but with increased attention; the prayer acquires a rhythm of its own and enters into the heart, working in the background and becoming unceasing; the words are "Jesus Christ, Son of God, Saviour, have mercy on me, a sinner".

The next rung on the ladder to spiritual truth after meditation was seen in most religions as contemplation, defined as the cultivation of a general awareness of the spirit's action and presence in daily life; the spirit shows the contemplative where and when to be thankful, ways in which the spirit has sought to communicate, and where grace and guidance are needed for the next day. Many of the great spiritual writers suggest that such insights are preceded by periods of contemplation which involve absence, nothing-ness and darkness as these are states from which deep understanding of the ground of being is forged. This is perhaps best expressed in the words of the author of the *Tao Te Ching* (see the Appendix on Taoism):

There was something formless and perfect
before the universe was born.
It is serene. Empty. Solitary.
Unchanging. Infinite. Eternally present.
It is the mother of the universe.
For lack of a better name, I call it *Tao*.
It flows through all things,
inside and out, and returns,
to the origin of all things.[6]

Contemplative prayer leads to increased self-awareness, looking for the spirit's presence in all things, in conversations, desires, all we see, taste, hear and understand and in all our actions. A person whose life is always open to the spirit lives a life of prayer.

Communal prayer

If you are a spiritual person, you will want to set aside some of your time to acknowledge the work of the spirit in your life and to learn what the spirit is calling you to do with your life, your gifts, your resources and your relationships. To a great extent, this time can be spent alone in private prayer but the search for the spirit is not a personal one because how we relate to one another is as important as how we relate to the spirit. We need concrete involvement with a real community, its problems and its graces. The essence of the spirit focuses us on relationships and on how we can care for those in our family, among our friends, in our neighbourhood and in the wider world. This means that we cannot respond to the spirit only in private but must also do so in community with like-minded others. We need

6   No. 25 in an English translation of the "Tao Te Ching" by Stephen Mitchell (Harper and Row, New York, 1988)

to spend time with them sharing our beliefs, experiences, fears, joys and concerns; and we need to do so in a group or groups which bring together a diverse mix of people, not all of whom we will like but all of whom we are called to love. Usually (in a religious sense) such gatherings are called meeting for worship.

So what do is meant by worship? At its root the word 'worship' comes from the word 'worth' and to worship something or someone is to give them their worth. This involves taking time to recognise the worth or value of someone or something. If you 'worship' a pop idol, then you give them their worth to you by listening to them, spending time at concerts and learning about them. If you 'worship' a football team, you do so by going to matches to watch them or seeing games involving them on the television and by learning more about them. If you 'worship' your spouse, you do so by respecting and honouring him or her, doing things for them, and seeking the best for them at all times. In a similar way, if you worship the spirit which is alive in your heart, you will want to spend time listening, giving thanks, talking and committing to the work of the spirit along with others who share a similar understanding.

Different religions have different ways of conducting worship but prayers and reading the scripture (with or without exposition) are common to them all. In Islam, worshippers prostrate themselves for prayer led by the imam; in Hinduism and Buddhism, worshippers spend time sitting before or walking around a shrine, stopping to bow and say a prayer; in Judaism prayer is led by the rabbi and takes a traditional form; Christianity has many different forms of worship – Catholics kneel to follow a written liturgy; Orthodox stand for prayer, using the same liturgy for both corporate and private prayer; Protestants make more use of extempore prayer with the worshippers sitting or standing in accordance with their tradition. Sometimes prayers may be sung or chanted; some prayers are sufficiently well known for them to be recited by all of the worshippers; and many churches have prayer books which are used so that the worshippers can join in the prayers.

Those religions which have a strong scriptural basis (Judaism, Christianity and Islam) have full-time teachers, ministers or priests, supported in some cases by lay readers/preachers, who arrange for the scriptures to be read and then offer, from their studies and experience, an exposition of particular passages and their relevance to the worshippers. Particular churches or denominations have what is known as a lectionary which governs the passages to be read in public worship so that the whole of the scriptures is covered over a set period.

Worship also includes the singing of hymns, interpretations through dance and drama, modern religious or secular music, clips from films and television, artwork such as paintings, sculptures, mosaics, stained glass, flowers, incense and elaborate ritual, including beautiful coloured robes worn by the priest or minister. All of these are ways of involving the worshippers in the celebration of the power of the spirit in their lives.

Learning and practising

Part of worship is sharing with others our experience of trying to live a spiritual life. This involves learning from others and telling to others. In those religions which have a strong scriptural base, worship almost always includes a period of teaching and encouragement. In some cases individual worshippers are encouraged to speak about their own experiences as a means of reassurance and inspiration for others. These elements are intended to provide greater understanding of the mystery which the spiritual life involves. Clearly today it is possible for more people to read the scriptures and commentaries for themselves but until relatively recently (and still in some parts of the world) large numbers of people were illiterate and the service of worship was an occasion to teach about the religion.

Worship, however, is as much about practice as about gathering from time to time with others to express a commitment to a particular spirit-filled worldview. The truth of the spiritual life is found not so much in the expositions of the learned scholar or the beautiful cadences of the prayer book as in the attempts by ordinary people to put it into practice. The teachings of the spirit will lead us to behave in particular ways and they will be reinforced if we find that they work for us; indeed it is by finding the truth of our commitment to spirit-led living that we come to worship because we want to celebrate the truth. Thus worship and practice are two sides of the same coin; the desire to worship arises out of practice and improved practice can be inspired by sharing in worship.

One of the issues for spiritual people today is discerning the truth that governs their lives. In the west we have been encouraged over the past century to be sceptical of authority and to test it before giving it credence. The authority of the police, doctors, priests, teachers, journalists, experts and so on has been undermined by raised educational achievement, increased knowledge of shortcomings in authoritative advice (manifested in serious errors, evidence of self-interest, and instances of unethical behaviour), and greater access to information (e.g. through the internet). In the west (and increasingly throughout the world) people are not prepared to accept without questioning the pronouncements of anyone in supposed authority. Thus, those who claim to have the answers to spiritual questions, such as ministers of religion, find themselves either operating in a period of decline because people are no longer interested in listening to their pronouncements or having to adjust and create situations in which people can debate and discuss their claims. The preaching side of worship and the reliance on scriptural authenticity are under threat; more opportunity has to be given to debating rather than being told. Thus the part of worship which is about listening to others and sharing with them has to be given greater prominence in line with experience-led belief.

The spirit at the centre of our lives wants us to celebrate in worship by creating and admiring. All of us are given talents which we use to create things, atmospheres and relationships. Worship of the spirit, it seems to me, should be the opportunity to admire what others have created and together to create new things. Admiring is the process of learning from others and their achievements; so we might admire a cake or a painting or a voice or a thought or a patchwork quilt or an action or a game or a television programme; and from these we acquire ideas for ourselves of things that we might do. Creating is working together on something that the worshipping community thinks is worthwhile. It might include such things as writing a prayer, composing a song, producing a banner, arranging a display of flowers, organising a concert, planning a party or organising a welcome event. All of these are elements of worship; they are a response to being filled with the spirit. They should be approached worshipfully and included in worship.

Some religions have been hostile to enjoyment, thinking that what God wants are serious and miserable people, conscious of their own imperfections and seeking righteousness in a dour, joyless life. Nothing could be further from the truth of the spirit, which rejoices in the created world, takes pleasure in laughter and happiness, looks for the best in people and wants them to enjoy life, and has no time for concepts like 'original sin'. The spirit teaches us that we were born into a good world as inherently good people whose purpose is to enjoy life, caring for others and for the world in which we live. Some of us lose that vision and see our lives as devoted to personal aggrandisement, at the expense of others; some of us are overcome by illness, natural disaster or ill-treatment by others so that they lose that sense of purpose; others become so bitter as a result of their early upbringing or personal circumstances that they cannot see how to recover by simply giving themselves to the care of others. But none of these experiences deny the truth that we are here to enjoy ourselves.

We should expect worship, therefore, to be enjoyable and to have elements that make us feel happy alongside more serious elements that remind us of our responsibilities to the spirit and to one another. Elements that are enjoyable include music, song, dancing, jokes, stories, laughing, smiling, being involved, clapping, celebrating achievements, eating, chatting and being with other people at ease with themselves. If this sounds more like going to the theatre or cinema than to worship, then that is good because we should think of the things and places and happenings that give us pleasure and try to replicate them in worship events.

Engaging in ritual and sacrament

Two other aspects of worship which are very important to humans have emerged from the history of religions. They are ritual and sacrament. Ritual is about having special words and actions to celebrate the high points of human living such as birth, naming, commitment, marriage, partnership, redundancy, change, leaving or arriving in the community, illness and death. Sacrament is about having special words and actions to remind people of the spiritual side of living. All religions have recognisably similar rituals; their sacraments vary enormously because they reflect their theologies; sometimes the sacraments are part of rituals (e.g. the sacrament of baptism as part of a naming ritual or vice-versa or the sacrament of holy matrimony as part of a marriage ritual).

Ritual is important to remind us of our humanity - the stages through which we go as growing and aging human beings. We share most of them in common and so it is good to take time out to get together to celebrate them. In the past rituals have tended to reflect the exclusiveness of most religions and have been available only to those who conformed with the particular religion's entry requirements e.g. you could only have a naming ceremony for a child in Christian countries if it involved baptism into the church. Today there is much greater flexibility both inside and outside religions; religions have begun to realise that they have to become more open (e.g. ordaining female priests, marrying divorced people, blessing same-sex partnerships) though the openness is only slowly emerging and is being resisted by the traditionalist wing of all religions; and outside the church there are many more opportunities for people to engage in ritual (e.g. civil weddings, recognition of same-sex partnerships, green burials). Those whose lives are led by the spirit should look to organise and participate in celebrations of the major events of human life as recognitions of the joy of being alive, of commitment to one another and of the value of life.

Sacraments are more specific to religions and are more concerned with building barriers and reinforcing belief than celebrating life and all it means. An example is the Christian sacrament of the Eucharist (also known as The Lord's Supper, the Divine Liturgy, Holy Communion and the Mass). In the early Christian church the Eucharist was considered to be the highest expression of community. Through the breaking of bread and the serving of wine, the life, death and resurrection of Jesus were remembered, re-enacted and proclaimed. All participated in the shared meal and the focus was on forgiveness, grace and compassion. It was both a contemplation on the mystery of God and a commitment to a way of life as 'ambassadors of Christ', as Christ is received in the midst of the church – a public event,

149

not private. The Eucharist became the core of Christian liturgy which emerged slowly as doctrine and practice was developed. The Eucharist is a very powerful sacrament for building the Christian church as people come together regularly to participate in a commemorative ritual which in some denominations is seen also to have mystical power. Even those who doubt aspects such as transubstantiation can testify to the power of the Eucharist in encouraging believers to be open to receive God's gifts, with others from different/diverse backgrounds, to recognise their inter-relatedness, to give thanks and to share with the world, especially the hungry and poor; it points the way to new life in Jesus. However, as a sacrament, it only makes sense to those who are Christians; it is a religious act coming out of a particular religion.

Some points to consider

1. Many people who are not religious pray. Why do they do so? To whom do they address their prayers?
2. Does the discussion of how you think of the spirit help to clarify for you how you might pray and what you might ask for?
3. You may be familiar with talking prayers but less so with listening prayers. How might your spiritual understanding increase through listening?
4. If you do not regularly attend acts of worship, do you feel a desire to do so? If so, what deters you?
5. What are the reasons why ritual and sacrament are important to human beings? Give some examples.

11. Living with pain, suffering and death

Ever since life began on earth human beings have pondered the mystery of pain, suffering and death. Some of the questions that we ask are why do some people seem to suffer much more than others, why does the experience of severe pain seem to be something of a lottery, why do some people die prematurely and what happens to us when we die. All of the world's religions set out to address these questions and they have very different answers. Some see pain and suffering as a punishment which comes to those who live their lives selfishly and unjustly, ignoring God's laws; this is a reflection of the human desire to see some form of external justice. Some make a promise of life beyond death in a place called heaven to those who embrace God's teaching whilst condemning those who don't to eternal damnation in a place called hell. And some suggest that our lives are cyclical and that we can improve our lot in the next life by living better in our current life. These various answers are now recognised as being simply myths, stories which offer a picture of what perhaps we would like to happen. Let us move on from those stories and explore what we can really say about pain, suffering and death from a spiritual perspective.

Some principles

The first general point to make is that pain, suffering and death are universal (i.e. they come to all of us) though some endure more pain and more suffering than others.

The second overall point is that human beings are complex. The sources of pain and suffering are many – physical, emotional, psychological, social and spiritual. As we have learned more about the human make-up, we have realised that all these elements are inter-related and often more than one is the cause. For example, physical illness can be an outcome of an emotional problem caused by a break-up in a relationship. Those to whom we entrust the care of our human condition, whether doctors, psychiatrists, social workers, therapist or priests, have to take a holistic view of the individual rather than diagnosing in a narrow area of expertise.

Thirdly, many experiences of pain and suffering could be alleviated if not eradicated if politically we chose to make the funds available. There is no reason why people should die of hunger anywhere in the world because there could be enough food to go round if we chose to allocate resources for this purpose. Similarly the impact of diseases which kill prematurely such as typhoid, cancer, heart disease etc. could be greatly reduced if we chose to invest in their eradication throughout our world. And there is no reason why people anywhere should suffer from Aids if we made the drugs available to all in need at low cost. And so on. It is within the ability of humankind to alleviate suffering if governments and electorates cared sufficiently.

Linked to this point is the fact that much of the pain, suffering and death on our planet arises at times of warfare. You may question whether it is possible to eradicate fighting and violence completely but there is no doubt that much of it is unnecessary. Some attempt to justify war on the grounds of self-defence and use various arguments for just wars but there is a big question-mark over whether killing is ever justifiable and certainly many wars that we have seen in the recent past have achieved nothing other than the death and suffering of large numbers of innocent people.

A fourth consideration is that some pain, suffering and death arises from unforeseen causes such as traffic accidents, electrical faults, earthquakes, storms and flooding. Some insurance companies call the last three of these acts of God; it is difficult to imagine a more ridiculous explanation! They are part of our human existence and in recent times we have devoted a lot of energy to trying to reduce the likelihood of accidents through the introduction of safety standards, professionalization of those engaged in installing and maintaining dangerous systems, and general improvements in design and manufacture of products. All of these improvements need to be spread around the world so that more people can benefit from them. But at the end of the day we live in a world that involves risk and no-one can escape the possibility of some form of accident which leads to pain, suffering or death.

Fifthly, the question of why some people seem to endure more pain and suffering than others cannot really be answered; it is one of the mysteries of life. Medical research is continually finding explanations and treatments for life threatening conditions which a few years ago were untreatable. This is a sign that our advances in knowledge are explaining and ameliorating medical conditions year by year. On the other hand, doctors are quite ready to admit that not everything can be explained or diagnosed and that some things will always remain a mystery. For example, some people for no apparent reason react much better to a form of treatment than others. This is because each of us is unique as a human being and the complex mix of our make-up operates uniquely for each one of us.

Finally it must be stressed in a book on the spiritual understanding of life that pain and suffering are not handed to people by an all-powerful God for some vindictive or judgemental reason; such a God does not exist. Nor can we ask God to intervene and take them away by some supernatural means; such an intervening God does not exist. That is not to say, however, that we cannot use the spiritual understanding of life to improve our own experience of pain and suffering and to ease that of others.

The role of the spirit in dealing with pain and suffering

Let us think about the spiritual outlook on pain and suffering from a personal perspective first. It will be clear from what has been said so far that the spiritual understanding of life takes as a starting point the existence of a soul whose role in each of our lives is to sharpen our desire to be alive, to sensitise us to the non-material joys of living, to enable us to understand our existence and to provide balance and integrity in all that we do. This results for people who embrace this vision in an approach to life which removes anxiety, nurtures wisdom and gives perspective. Such a person is not cast adrift by the day-to-day ups-and-downs of life but is able to deal with them calmly and intelligently. This means that when a problem arises, whether personal, financial, medical, social, technical or of any other kind, his or her reaction is positive and reflective, with no sense of being overwhelmed, frightened or unable to cope. This enables him or her to put the pain and suffering into perspective; it does not mean that he or she does not feel the pain or feel the suffering, but it does mean that capacity for thought and action is not lost. It is simply another situation that needs to be reflected on and handled in as balanced and honest a way as possible. Usually the spiritual person survives what life throws at him or her with equanimity.

Let us now turn to the spiritual outlook on the pain and suffering of others. When it comes to the pain and suffering of others, the spiritual person will offer practical action and empathy. Practical action is of prime importance and the first task is to find ways of alleviating the pain through whatever appropriate means, usually by getting medical help; such action is the natural response of one human being to another who is in need; walking by on the other side is never an appropriate spiritual reaction. Empathy is about being alongside the person who is suffering and trying to understand what they are experiencing. It is about opening the eyes of our heart to appreciate more fully the suffering of the other. Very often it is simply about listening and offering sympathetic responses; sometimes this is called compassionate solidarity, a way of saying that you know that you cannot take the pain away but you want to be with the sufferer in the midst of it. It is not usually about telling the person what to do (e.g. snap out of it) though occasionally ways of alleviating the stress become apparent and should be offered for their consideration. The spiritual person will usually have an holistic view of human problems and will not jump too quickly to an inappropriate explanation of the problem without weighing up all the possibilities. People who are undergoing difficult times in their lives for whatever reason have need of both carers with expertise that may help them (e.g. doctors, therapists, counsellors etc.) and carers whose are there to support them and seek the best for them as fellow human beings. The spiritual person fulfils the latter role, though he or she may also be a person with relevant expertise as well.

One of the key ways of helping people in any situation is being able to see them as they really are, ordinary human beings like you and me seeking the best for themselves and for others. If we are able to adopt such an outlook we are much more likely to be able to help them because we are not approaching them with preconceived ideas/prejudices. Such an outlook is a spiritual one. It is about not making things worse for people. Not long ago people who were ill were kept apart even from their family; we have now realised the importance of love in healing. Today many people suffer because they feel left out perhaps as a result of a disease or a physical disability or the colour of their skin or their religious faith. There are lots of people in our world, in our country and in our town who feel lonely, left out, and frightened. Some people cry themselves to sleep and wake up afraid of the day ahead. It is very easy today for people to feel rejected and isolated and it is a miserable feeling; whether they are there through their own fault or through circumstances beyond their control, it is a bleak, painful place to be. The job of the spiritual person is to love and care for those in need, the rejected, isolated, hurting or depressed.

Finally it is very important to the spiritual understanding of pain and suffering to recognise the importance of forgiveness. Much day-to-day suffering stems from a sense of guilt about things that we have done which are wrong. A wonderful feeling of freedom and lightness comes when we finally get round to admitting when we have gone wrong. Such admission is essential so that we can do something about it and sort it out. People often live false lives, pretending that all is well, whilst feeling troubled about something that they have done. They need the opportunity to stop deceiving themselves and they need a sympathetic person who will listen to them non-judgementally. The spiritual person who seeks to live an honest life can help to free people from the pain of living a lie.

The Buddha urged his disciples to be rooted in the spirit so that they would not be overcome by pain and suffering; rather they would look suffering in the face, sit down with it, transform it and move beyond; they would look deeply at the causes of suffering and seek to tackle them; and they would love those who are suffering, not in a generic way (you cannot love in general) but by loving the suffering person right here and right now.

The role of the spirit in our thinking about death

One of the common features of all religions is that they try to offer an explanation of what happens when we die. This question is at the forefront of the minds of human beings, especially as they approach their own death, or when their loved ones die or when a young person dies before their time. How does the spiritual person answer this question?

All living human beings want to know why they are alive and whether they will have any sort of existence when they are no longer alive. This is because we tend to think of life as finite, beginning at birth and ending at death. As a result many of us are short-term in our focus (e.g. 'enjoy life whilst you have it', 'I'm alright, Jack', 'eat drink and be merry', 'live for the moment', 'spend, spend, spend') and are unable to lift our eyes above having sufficient material possessions to have a good time. Thus in the west we are at the whim of the fashions of the consumer society, in which having the 'right' trainers, handbag, car or perfume dominates our thinking. If we did not feel that our lives were short-term, we might take a different, more spiritual approach to them.

For example, if we see our lives as having closer connections with the past (before our birth) and into the future (after our physical death), our perspective is broadened and we think less about the short-term. Similarly, if we think less about our own situation and more about others' needs, we help the human race as a whole to have fuller and richer lives. The spirit is planted in our hearts at birth and our life has a component which has existed from before our birth and will continue to exist long after we have died. In all of these ways of thinking the immediate is less important than the eternal. If through the spirit we can adopt this frame of mind our natural concern about death is removed because our spirits are part of the eternity of God. We cannot know the precise form in which eternity operates because our minds and bodies are finite and incapable of thinking in infinite terms but we can be sure that we are part of what has always existed and always will.

This form of eternal life is not to be pictured in human terms (e.g. in angelic form, in a garden paradise or in the fires of hell) but in spiritual terms. Many people have the idea (spread abroad by religions) that after death they will arrive either in heaven (if they have lived a good life) or in hell (if they have lived a bad life) and pictures have been painted of these two locations. The suggestion that there might be two locations arises from the human desire to see bad/evil people punished after death and good people (like themselves) rewarded. Thus the concept is a human projection without any evidence (whether scientific, experiential or psychological) to support it. After death, when all our human senses have decayed and ceased to operate, we will not have any human sensations (i.e. be able to see, hear, touch, taste, speak). Any existence beyond death will not take material form.

Everything about death looks final. The body that we knew laughing, angry, anxious or intrigued is still; all the memories that our loved one had are locked inside and out of our reach. It seems to be the end of responding, thinking, feeling and moving. Clustered around it are other endings; the cupboards to be cleared, possessions and clothing now redundant; terrible gaps in family, in friendships, in rotas, in committees. The tragedy of death is its terrible finality; it is like a violent rejection of what was previously so very much alive, a slap in the face to life itself. It need not be like that. If we see ourselves as passing through phases of existence, then death is a transition point just as birth is. So, except when death comes suddenly at a young age, we can prepare, and help others to prepare, for the transition.

Many people want to know whether they will be recognisable after death and whether they will recognise their loved ones who have gone before. The answer to neither question is yes in the terms in which they are posed. People think in bodily terms because that is what their material life encourages them to do. It is much more realistic to think about this in a non-material, spiritual way. Spiritually we never lose someone who has died if we have loved them deeply, any more than they lose us when we die of our material existence. They may have died, leaving you to mourn them, to wish they were still sharing life in all its ups-and-downs with you. But you never lose them because something of their spirit is within you.

My belief is that the soul is the place where part of the spirit of God lives within us; it comes to us in the being born process, remains with us through our life and never dies. Our soul is where the spirit finds its resting place within us just as the souls of other people during their lives also host the spirit. It is possible for spiritual people who understand prayer to spend time communicating with the spirit of a loved one who has died. How? If we spend time building into our own lives the lovely features of a loved one's life, then they are spiritually with us all of the time. If we visit places where they loved to go and which were important to them spiritually, then they are again sharing our lives. If we bring to mind those parts of their life where their soul was most distinctly at work and spend time there, then we will find ourselves fully in contact with them again. We need to think about what they enjoyed doing – crossword puzzles, walking in the Lake District, playing cards with friends, hosting a meal, campaigning for trade justice – and spend time with them in furthering that activity. Then we will know them close to us.

If we think of our earthly life as a finite, physical place (e.g. a circle) which we enter by being born and within which we do the normal things that humans do - eat, plan, work, talk, make friends, watch TV, learn things etc. After a finite, physical time period we leave this circle by being born backwards (i.e. dying). When we die our spirit is no longer in the finite, physical place; instead it participates in the infinite, non-material, eternal spiritual world, which is immeasurably bigger than we have ever imagined, if all we have known is physical, material life inside the circle. Outside the circle is the whole outdoors, stretching outwards and upwards, and full of light and colour, better than anything we could ever imagine if all we had known was the circle of life. Just as the circle is not the only place, so this life is not all there is. There is an infinite spiritual world outside the circle and when we reach the point of our death, our spirit will rejoin that spiritual world.

I believe that our spirit is part of the universal spirit of humanity which comprises the spirits of all people who have ever lived and whoever will live. Our spirit has learnt from those who have gone before and will provide wisdom for those who come afterwards. In that sense it continues beyond death. Our spirit does not survive in a personal sense other than through the people who have known us and love and cherish us beyond our death.

Some points to consider

1. At the start of this chapter six principles are discussed to put the later discussion in context. Do you agree with them all? If not, which do you disagree with and why?
2. Does the discussion of the spiritual person's approach to pain and suffering help you – personally and in relation to others? If not, why not? Have you examples to share?
3. The chapter makes the point that forgiving and being forgiven are important to healing. Does this ring true in your experience? Why?
4. Does the explanation of what happens when we die help or hinder you? In either case, try to explain why.
5. Can you through examples elaborate the

discussion of how we can prepare ourselves and others for death?

6. Do the final two paragraphs make sense for you or do you think of life after death in physical/ materially recognisable terms? Why?

PART 3

Christianity as my vehicle for spiritual living

12. The essence of Christianity

I mentioned at the beginning of the book that I express my spirituality through my Christian faith and that I proposed to discuss this at the end of the book as a way of illustrating life in the spirit. The trouble with mentioning the word Christianity is that the reader may jump immediately to assumptions about what I believe or may be put off reading this last chapter. Please do not do either! I plan to cover four topics: how I came to be involved in Christianity; ways in which the institutional church gets in the way of the spirit and needs to change; ways in which over the centuries Christianity has been made more complex by theologians than it needs to be and what needs to be discarded; and how following Jesus can provide riches of life in the spirit.

How I became involved in Christianity

I was not in any strong sense brought up in a Christian family. My father was an agnostic. The hypocrisy of professing Christians raised doubts for him but what really turned him against the church was the idea it promotes of an all-powerful God who appeared to have allowed/approved the slaughter of millions of innocent men in the first world war, the growth of the Nazi regime in Germany and the devastations of the second war. But he did not in any way, other than in occasional arguments later in his life, try to influence his sons. My mother was better disposed to the church but more as a helper (e.g. raising money for the Scouts) than as a believer; she rarely attended services of worship. Occasionally I was sent to Sunday School classes but never with any sense of commitment or indeed any long-term involvement. Thus I was more aware of the teachings of Christianity from the religious education lessons at school than from Sunday School attendance, and sadly my experience of sitting in RE lessons reading (without much explanation) long passages of the Old and New Testaments left me cold.

However, when I reached the age of wanting to spend more time with members of the opposite sex (in my case I was 16), my friends encouraged me to go to the local Methodist Church where the youth club was considered to be the best and there were plenty of lovely girls. I was now on the periphery of the church and I took on various tasks (e.g. participating in a few services of worship, editing a magazine) when asked by people for whom I had a high regard. But I was not a believer in any sense. I went away to University and after an abortive attempt to make friends through the Methodist Society my involvement with the local churches never took off. However, in the meantime I became engaged to one of the girls from the youth club who regularly attended the church and, when at home, I attended with her, still rather sceptical and not entirely at ease. We married and moved away; she joined the local Methodist church and challenged the minister to come round and see me to try to persuade me to join. She told him that it would not be easy! However, I found myself in tune with his social and political views and I went to listen to him preaching. Within a short time I was helping with the youth club, attending a house group and doing all sorts of caring activities in the town (e.g. decorating houses for old people, working with homeless men). The experience of trying to live Jesus' way made me feel that there was a truth and freedom in the Christian faith which I had not found elsewhere. I was asked also to help with the Junior Church and the preparation of lessons forced me to read and become familiar with the scriptures. Before long I felt sufficiently committed to become a member of the church and after about five years felt a call to preach. Since then I have expressed my spirituality through the Christian Church – but not without many misgivings.

Problems of the church as an institution

There is no such thing as 'the church'; there are many churches with many differing beliefs and practices. Despite this I am going to make some broad generalisations in this section, using the word 'church', in a generic sense. Clearly not all of them apply to every church but the general points are true to some extent of all churches.

The main problem (some would say virtue) of the church is that it is made up of human beings! When human beings form an organisation, they tend fairly quickly to set boundaries to exclude those whom they do not want as members and then some members start to vie with one another for positions of power within the organisation. We have all seen it - in school, at work, in the club, in political parties, even in families. It seems that people want to have around them those that they like and who think the same way as them; and then certain people want to dominate, others are happy for them to do so, and a few resent it. The first Christian groups tried to follow Christ's teaching and to avoid these problems; they welcomed all, they had shared leadership and the only requirement for membership was to commit to Jesus' way. But this did not last for long, as far as we can tell from Paul's letters in the New Testament; people started to argue about who could be a member, what they had to believe and who could determine these matters. So the early church succumbed to human failings (hardly surprising!); it became dogmatic about what people had to believe in order to be a member, excluded those who did not agree, and even persecuted those who challenged the agreed dogma. And all of this happened in an organisation whose avowed aim was to celebrate Jesus Christ, one whose clearest teachings was about inclusiveness. It is hardly surprising that some churches today are seen by outsiders as private clubs for those with extreme views about life, and I find it sad that some church leaders are unable to loosen the reins and take steps to be organisationally more inclusive.

This human organisation had two other problems from the early days. The first was that, although Jesus Christ is recorded as treating all people in the same way, the leaders (all men) treated women as inferior and did not allow them (with few exceptions) into positions of authority. This was a reflection of society at the time when women were seen but not heard, given the menial tasks around the home and not allowed to mix with male society, but it led to a situation in which women apparently had little role in the church, its doctrines and its liturgy. Not only is this regrettable because the feminine contribution to interpretation and creativity was largely ignored but it is the origin of the conflicts that have divided churches in the past 100 years as campaigns for the ordination of women have gathered momentum.

It is a matter of great concern to me and to many that the church is so steeped in the dominance of the male sex - from the attribution of male characteristics to God to the assumption inherent in scripture and doctrine that the female is somehow inferior. The language of the Bible, the approach of the vast majority of hymns and prayers in current use and the almost universal reference to God as he are real problems for many involved in Christian worship. It sometimes seems that male clergy are reluctant to deal with issues of language and the need for change. They seem unable to see that the all-pervading idea that male is the norm is at the heart of many current problems of abuse, violence and injustice towards women, the disempowerment of women in many societies across the world, and their lack of personal development opportunities. At the very least

Christians should follow Jesus' teachings on love, dignity and equality and stand against the many ways in which women suffer indifference, contempt, hostility and exclusion in society in general and in some churches in particular.

The second problem was that the new organisation found itself in a position of power and wealth in society as more people gave it their allegiance and eventually the Roman emperor Constantine (for political reasons) made Christianity the official religion of the empire. We all know that power and wealth corrupt; in our day, especially in the political arena, we can identify people of apparent honesty and courage succumbing to the desire to control others and to amass unnecessary wealth. So it was within the church; whether we think of the Pope in Rome or monastic foundations or local priests, many seem to have craved power and sought material wealth. And all of this despite the fact that Jesus taught his followers to seek the lowest place and to set aside material gain for the sake of the kingdom of God. A starker example of the human failings of the church cannot be found – except perhaps that the church over two millennia has been at the centre of some terrible and violent wars, making no effort to promote Jesus' way of non-violence.

The most frightening aspect of the church's apparent rejection of Jesus' teachings can be found in its efforts to force people into belief. Once the church had a set of doctrines, those who disagreed even with the smallest element were treated as heretics and violently dealt with. The period of the inquisition, the burning of so-called witches and the exclusion of non-believers from advancement are examples of the ruthless treatment which the church handed out to those who were not on its side. With those who were completely outside because they subscribed to another religion, the church was even more ruthless – think of the crusades against the Muslims, the ghettoisation of Jews (eventually leading, some would say, to the Nazi atrocities against the Jews), the treatment of 'conquered' peoples by the various 'global empires' in the name of Christianity (e.g. the violent Spanish conquest of the Americas, the British treatment of indigenous people all over the world). All this was done in the name of Christ (what a distortion of his teaching!) and to maintain control in order to preserve and increase wealth and power.

Sadly the church is not renowned for justice, and this is another condemnation of the church as an institution. Although, in its name, systems of justice were instituted, schools and colleges started and nursing and health care developed, the church has often been seen as self-interested, only doing the things which maintained its power base. When we look around today, we do not see much evidence of the church seeking politically to end wars, remove the threat of famine or give all people everywhere access to education. What we see instead are huge amounts of effort put into stopping people from using contraceptives, campaigning against abortion, preventing child-abuse cases within the church from being dealt with in an open way, rejecting the ordination of women and condemning homosexuality. All of this is negative, a denial of justice to the poor, the marginalised and the weak; and who did Jesus seek to welcome into God's kingdom but the poor, the marginalised and the weak? The church seems to want to close ranks and to exclude; Jesus always wanted to draw in those who were being treated unjustly.

Some argue that little of Christ's teaching is in practice seen in the church as an organisation and this is what has caused them to reject the teaching of Jesus Christ. I am sure that if he saw some of the things that have been done in his name, he would be horrified. This is not to say, however, that no Christ-like things have been done; many wonderful things have been done and continue to be done by millions of individuals who follow Christ's teachings.

I want to finish this section by saying something about the way in which the church has treated the Bible and Jesus Christ; this will explain some of the behaviour that we have been considering. In the early centuries of the church, the Christian religion was under threat from many different places. There were pre-existing religions (such as Judaism) which challenged the whole basis for Christianity; there were intellectuals throughout the Mediterranean lands who found the emerging faith in a risen saviour to be quite incredible; and within the church arguments were raging about how the Old and New Testaments were to be interpreted and over points of theology. When Constantine decided to make Christianity the official religion of the Roman empire, he saw these disagreements as potentially divisive in the unified empire. So he ensured that the church closed ranks and leaned on the key leaders to decide what members of the Christian church were to believe about the Bible and about Jesus; they saw this as necessary to protect the church and enable it to grow; and these decisions by human beings (some of whom had considerable intellectual powers) continue to haunt the church even today when we have so much more knowledge of the way that the world works.

Thus parts of the church have decreed that the Bible is the divine and infallible word of God, despite the obvious errors, contradictions and impossibility of some passages; some concessions have been made to scholarship here and there, but the basic position for many churches remains that the Bible is literally true because it comes from God. They have signed up to literal interpretation of the Bible, despite the fact that it was written by human beings in their own context, at particular points in time, when knowledge of the world was very limited. Some parts of the church take a more liberal view and allow modern interpretation, but the Bible's records of creation, the survival of Noah and his family after the flood, the virgin birth, Christ's resurrection and the prospect of a second coming are largely regarded as literally correct. Moreover, the church sees the Bible as the revelation (in some cases the final revelation) of God's will for his people; there has been some acceptance that revelation is ongoing and that it needs to be re-interpreted from age to age; but in the main the church goes back to the Bible to discover God's will on controversial issues such as evolution, contraception, abortion, genetic engineering, weapons of mass destruction, none of which, of course, are explicitly referenced in the Bible.

This approach to the Bible is simply unacceptable to people today, like me, who have been brought up to challenge for authenticity, to search for evidence, to be aware of scientific and technological developments and to read about psychological and sociological interpretation of behaviour. Today when there is an expectation that people should deal with the Bible intelligently and with integrity, sadly large parts of the church are trapped in outmoded and untenable ideas that do not recognise the developments in human thinking. Perhaps 150 years ago when levels of literacy were much lower, one could understand the lack of challenge to the church's approach, but today it cannot be excused for taking a head in the sand approach to scripture.

My view is that the Bible was written over a period of about a thousand years by various members of the Hebrew people and the early Christian church i.e. by human beings inspired by their experience of God's spirit. It tells us about their experiences, how they interpreted them, how God was involved in their lives and how they responded. It is their witness to God - not God's witness to God. Thus the Bible is not God's revealed truth but people's interpretation of it in their particular time and place; it uses the language and concepts of the cultures in which it emerged. The Bible is central to the Christian faith and is sacred not because it is of divine origin but because the Old Testament provides the background which enables us to interpret the teachings of Jesus and the early church, the New Testament tells the story of Jesus and how his message was carried forward, and the Bible as a whole provides the basis for the Christian world-view. It is not infallible, not totally accurate and not literally true. It is not science and it is not history as we know it today. None of this means that it is not true.

Thus, when we read the Bible, our approach should be based on careful study (making wide use of the work of scholarship), draw on the tradition of Christians through the centuries, and take account of our and others' experience of God working with his people. Above all, our approach must make use of our intellect which God has given to us. In order for us to understand the Bible, it is essential that scholars provide the Christian community with accurate historical explanation of life at the times when the different books were written, of contemporary, related literature and of the inter-relationship of different parts of the Bible (e.g. how a Gospel writer like Matthew drew heavily on the Old Testament scripture in building his picture of Jesus). Such historical analysis can offer commentary on whether something actually happened but this is less important because incidents are often included in the Biblical record to make a point or to support an interpretation rather than because they actually happened at that point in time in that place involving those specific people. This is because much of the Bible is a metaphorical rather than historical document. Metaphor is a way of seeing: "look at it like this". If it speaks of God's hands and feet, it is pointing towards the idea of relating to God as a person rather than asserting that God does have hands and feet! Similarly the creation stories in Genesis or the Virgin birth stories in Luke should not be seen as historically accurate; they are pointing to profound truths (i.e. in these cases, the continuous, dynamic creativity of God and the presence of God in Jesus' birth). Saying that the Bible is largely a metaphorical document does not detract from its sacred role; stories carry profound truths even if they are not factual reports. Some people confuse truth with facts; they think that if stories are not factual they cannot be true. Clearly this is nonsensical.

Unfortunately the sorry tale of the church's approach to the Bible has parallels in the way in which it has dealt with Jesus. The church leaders formulated creeds (statements of what Christians believed) which declared him to be:

- the Son of God (because his divinity was challenged from the beginning by the Jews),
- the Messiah (because he was a Jew and the Jews believed a coming Saviour or Messiah),
- born of a virgin (an addition to the historical record because they believed it enhanced his divinity),
- capable of miracles (which were stressed in order to convince people of his divine powers),
- chosen to die for our sins (raising all sorts of theological problems but offering an explanation of his death),
- raised from the dead (another sign of his divinity),
- seated at the right hand of God in heaven (a sign of his power in a realm far removed from us), and
- the only way to salvation (so as to emphasise Christianity as the only route to God).

All of these claims have some basis in the New Testament; of course, in many ways the New Testament was gathered and edited to support the case; but they are also capable of being challenged using the same source. For example, it is doubtful whether Jesus ever called himself the Son of God; the virgin birth appears in only one of the four gospels; the explanation of his death appears in Paul's letters, not in the gospels; and so on. Sadly the creeds make no reference to what Jesus taught about the kingdom of God, about religious hypocrisy, about caring for the weak and oppressed, about loving your neighbour as much as you love God, about not accumulating wealth, about serving as the lowest of all and living a life of self-sacrifice. Yet I would say that these are the most important elements of following Jesus.

The development of a creed (what we believe) was needed partly so that people had something to sign up to. Its definition was carried out by well-meaning early church fathers who were trying to summarise their theology, but as an encapsulation of Christian belief it is open to debate and challenge. The church, however, has chosen even now to hold on to it in its original form.

Discarding accumulated doctrinal baggage

You will gather from the discussion in the previous section that I am not entirely happy with the church's behaviour! Moreover, I am very unhappy about some of the doctrinal baggage that has been accumulated over the years and which I believe no longer has any place in today's church. In fairness to the church, much of this was developed at times when people were challenging it over what it believed about various issues; a definitive position was needed. Sadly, however, there is an unwillingness (mainly as a result of what I wrote in the previous section about the way in which the Bible has been treated) to revisit these doctrines when the church's positions are challenged today. So we find ourselves encumbered with a number of doctrines that are no longer tenable. They include creation, original sin, life after death, heaven and hell, salvation, the meaning of Christ's death on the cross, resurrection, the picture of God, and the emphases of the Christian life. I will deal with just a few of these.

If we take creation, for example, there are two accounts of creation at the beginning of the Bible in the Book of Genesis. Setting aside the conflicts between the two accounts, what is regrettable is that those who believe that the Bible is the literal word of God cling to a belief that the Genesis account of God creating the world in six days is a literal description of the creation of the world. They are unwilling to recognise all of the scientific evidence which is emerging in greater detail year by year and which gives a realistic account of how the universe came into existence, how the earth was formed and how life came to the earth over many millions of years through a process of evolution. In the USA the so-called creationists are even trying to rewrite school syllabi so that the Genesis account is taught to children as the true account of creation. It is clear to most Christians, however, that the stories in Genesis are myths which tell us a truth, not the literal word of God. The account at the beginning of the Bible is surely intended to get across to people some fundamentally important ideas about the world in which we live, namely: that God is an eternal spirit whose existence is not time related; that the world was, and potentially can continue to be, created in the image of this God of love; that there is a fundamental interdependence between the natural world (oceans, mountains, atmosphere, plants), the animal world, and the human world: that human beings are placed on this earth to care for it as stewards rather than owners; that if we lose sight of this truth things will go wrong between people and for the future of the earth; and that the earth, created in God's image, is fundamentally a good place of great beauty, fertility and stability, in which human beings are given choices which can lead towards destruction or continuing creation; and that we should not be surprised that if we make destructive choices in our lives they will lead to disastrous consequences for us as individuals and us as the human community.

Turning to original sin, I can find little in the Bible which suggests that human beings are from birth full of sin and evil; indeed the opposite is true. The Genesis myth makes clear that God is pleased with the created world, including human beings, and Jesus sees the goodness in people and seeks at all times their well-being. Sadly the early church, especially Augustine, invented the idea of original sin in order to justify their idea that Christ came and died on a cross as a redeemer of people's sinfulness. There is no suggestion in the words of Jesus that he saw his death in these terms, but when the early church was forming it was in a world which thought in terms of sacrifice to propitiate hostile or angry gods. In all religions and in the practices of primitive peoples, the concept of sacrifice is strong. Animals, and people even, were sacrificed in order to get the gods on your side. The early Christians had to explain why the Son of God (as they described Jesus) died ingloriously on a cross as a common criminal. The explanation that emerged was one of sacrifice for sin. The bizarre idea that innocent children at birth are full of sin became part of the church's doctrine and eventually infant baptism became a necessary ritual as a symbolic washing away of the sin through (later) belief in Jesus. I believe that this doctrine of original sin has much to answer for in the life of the Christian church; it suggests that people should have a continuous sense of guilt from birth; it portrays people as basically evil rather than basically good; and it allowed the powerful to justify the destruction of those who were not Christians on the grounds that they were lost and without salvation other than through turning to belief in Jesus Christ. Even worse, the exposition of this doctrine by Augustine and others highlighted that it was Eve (the first woman) who caused the downfall of Adam (the first man) by persuading him to eat from the tree of knowledge; thus women have been treated as the weaker and more sinful sex by Christian leaders throughout the centuries, despite Christ's express teaching that all people are created equal in the sight of God and practical expression of this through his friendship with women and others who were at the time regarded as second-class. Pelagius, a British theologian, tried to challenge the doctrine of original sin during Augustine's life-time but through the power politics of the early church he was declared to be a heretic in order to preserve a doctrine that suited the powerful men who led the church.

The concept of original sin was a key doctrine in the early centuries of the church when the leaders used fear as the means of bringing people into the Christian fold. They were told that as sinful people they were destined for hell (the place of great conflagration in which sinners would be destroyed); to avoid this, they had to become Christians and turn away from sinful behaviour, with the promise of life in heaven. Such concepts were common in the religions of primitive peoples; goodness (however defined) would lead to life after death in paradise, whereas evilness (however defined) would lead to destruction in hell. (I put 'however defined' in brackets because interpretations of good behaviour varied from society to society and from time to time within the Christian church; for example, when the political church needed to increase its power through warfare or needed to get rid of its opponents through witch-burning, killing people was judged to be good behaviour despite Christ's clear injunction against such action.) Thus the primitive concept of reward for good behaviour, as determined by the church, became enshrined in the church's doctrine and heaven and hell remain strong ideas still today.

Heaven and hell were pictured as physical places; in the early days hell was beneath the flat earth and heaven was beyond the sky; when the world was shown to be a globe rather than a disc and when the exploration of space found that there was no dome above the earth beyond which heaven could be found, it was difficult to retain the original belief in physical domains. But the concept of reward and punishment based on ideas of God as an omnipotent, ruthless judge, portrayed in some parts of the Old Testament, continues to have a hold on Christians. Jesus, however, taught a very different picture of a God of love who, as in the lovely story of the Prodigal Son, forgives and forgives, never punishing, always hoping that the lost will be found and that the evil-doer will come back to original goodness. Although the teaching of the Old Testament was a major element in Jesus' interpretation of God, he relatively rarely emphasises the judgement of God compared to the number of times that he promotes the idea of a loving spirit, surrounding people with forgiveness and love and wanting them to enjoy life in all its goodness. Sadly too many people within the church still hold on to the old image of God as a tyrannical judge, ready to destroy and defeat.

When we look at the development of the New Testament and the emergent doctrines of the early church, we find other baggage that needs to be discarded. One such is the virgin birth. There is very little tangible evidence that Jesus saw himself as anything other than a human being with an extraordinary insight into the love of God. The idea that his mother was a virgin never occurs in his words, does not appear in two of the Gospels (Mark and John), probably is not in the third (Matthew – there is an argument over whether the word used means virgin or young girl), and is only in the fourth (Luke) as an element of one Jewish school of thought. The early church, however, felt the need to explain how Jesus could be God if he was born of human parents and so invented the idea that the birth was a miracle and that Mary his mother was a virgin who conceived by the power of God's spirit. The literalists would have us believe that this actually happened. Those who believe in the truth of myth see that this is a story intended to convey a point that

Jesus' closeness to God is eternal; he came in human form but filled with the spirit; eventually he died a human death but his spirit did not die; he is presented as the example to us all of how we are filled with God's spirit at birth, can live a life close to the spirit and on physical death our spirit returns to God. Thus the spirit is eternal.

Although I believe that Jesus was put to death on a cross (the common Roman method of execution for convicted criminals), I have difficulty subscribing to the explanation for this which the established church has offered over the centuries, that Jesus died as a sacrifice for the sins of the world so that through him people might find salvation. I find this difficult for many reasons. First, there is no suggestion in the recorded words of Jesus that he ever saw his death at the hands of the authorities, though it was inevitable, in these terms; rather he saw himself as a victim of human reluctance to see God in his terms; he did not want to die but death was the consequence of what he was doing (one might draw parallels with Gandhi or Martin Luther King Jr.). Second, if the church interpretation is correct, it paints a picture of God as inhumane, wishing the cruellest of possible deaths on his 'son'; this is not a God that I can trust. Third, the church's doctrine completely ignores the more likely explanation of Jesus' crucifixion, which is that he was a victim of political infighting and religious conservatism/ protectionism; Jesus was executed because he was seen as a threat to the self-satisfied status quo. Fourth, although Jesus does seem to have believed in some form of life after death, in common with others at that time, he does not make reference to it very often, nor does he see his teaching as offering this type of salvation; he is much more concerned to lead people to transformation in this life, bringing about the Kingdom of God on earth. Despite these reservations, I see the cross as a powerful image pointing to the level of injustice in our world, revealing that often the only way to truth is through pain and sacrifice and proclaiming that strength is to be found in weakness.

We should perhaps at this point turn to the doctrine of the resurrection, the most important of all the doctrines. The Gospels are ambiguous about what actually happened but it seems clear that a group of confused, anxious and frightened disciples, afraid for their lives as the Jewish authorities tried to stamp out the challenge of Jesus, had an experience which convinced them that Jesus was alive and available to them at all times. Whether their experience was of Jesus' physical body is doubtful because in the Gospel accounts Jesus appears and disappears at will, walks through locked doors and is simultaneously seen in distant locations. Here we have another myth which tells a truth, that the spirit is eternal, can be experienced by ordinary people and is a source of direction, meaning and purpose in life. There is no need to worry about whether Jesus miraculously survived physical death; what he did do was to convince his followers that his teaching about eternal life in the kingdom of God was so true that they were willing to give their lives to proclaim this message. When human beings think about life after death or attend the funeral of a loved one, the Christian message is that the essence of each individual (his or her spirit) is eternal; it came from God, was to a greater or lesser extent aware of God during physical embodiment, and it has returned to God. Jesus taught the idea of there being many rooms for people in God's house; this human expression conveys an everlasting truth that the spirit is eternal whilst physical existence is finite.

Following Jesus

You may be asking yourself why I practise my spirituality within a Christian setting, given the criticisms which I have made of the Christian church and its doctrinal baggage. The reason is that, in Christ's teaching about himself and about the way to find fulfilment in life, I find a vision which is consistent with my experience of life. When I look at the words of Jesus I find a radical call to a way of life which makes complete sense for me. Let me take you through some of those key messages.

1. Jesus refers to God as his father, someone so close that he can talk to him day by day and learn from him how to conduct himself. Of course, not everyone has a good experience of their father, but we all know what we would like that experience to be: intimate, close, comforting, strengthening, believing. This was Jesus' experience of the spirit working in his life, nurturing and directing him. Jesus speaks of God as a meaningful and timeless presence who provides a consistent vision of how life should be led. Jesus is open to this spirit, flowing through him and out of him. He acts as a conduit for us to understand the nature of God by opening up for us a wider vision of what humanity could be like.

2. Jesus teaches that nothing is more important to the spiritual life than to love the spirit within and to love our neighbours. Our neighbours include our enemies and those who hate, curse and mistreat us. The spirit within us is a spirit of love and it reveals itself most fully when we love with all our heart, mind, strength and soul. Jesus provides us with a dynamic and living vision of how life might be, seen through his eyes.

3. Jesus' teaching, life and death emphasise the importance of self-sacrifice rather than self-interest and giving rather than receiving as the means to grace. He teaches us a way of lifting ourselves out of materialism and self-absorption. Whilst the ideas of detachment and selflessness are common to most religions, only

one, Christianity, presents its teaching in the life of a person. Most use abstract ideas whereas in Christianity we can see in Jesus how this is to be achieved.

4. Jesus calls us to repentance. This means recognising that from time to time (or, in some cases, all the time) we live in a way that is inconsistent with the spirit of love within us, expressing our regret that this is happening and setting out in all sincerity to spend more time with the spirit so that our life is guided by the spirit in all that we do.

5. Jesus urges us to pray regularly (not in public to get the applause of others, but in private, intimately) so that we increase our sensitivity to the spirit's way. He encourages us to live in a close relationship with the spirit, by spending time observing, interpreting and responding to the spirit of love.

6. Jesus is concerned about the ways in which people demonstrate their religiosity through piety and ritual and he says that these are of no value if they do not reflect a loving attitude to God and neighbour in daily living. He is very critical of hypocrisy and excuse-making.

7. Jesus is concerned about the practical ways in which the spirit reveals love in our lives and so he offers lots of advice in direct teaching and through parables about what life in the spirit looks like:

- It calls for a simple life-style
- It is not concerned with status and position in society or family
- It does not seek material riches
- It shares possessions with those in need
- It treats all human beings equally as children of the spirit

- It pursues healing and reconciliation
- It never uses violence
- It works at <u>making</u> peace
- It does not seek revenge but turns the other cheek and walks the extra mile
- It does not judge but is forgiving and merciful
- It cares for widows, orphans and the outcast
- It never rejects anyone regardless of how they have behaved
- It spends time seeking to restore those who are lost into a full relationship with the spirit
- It is passionate about social justice
- It speaks out when it sees behaviour or policies or words which are lacking in humility, justice, freedom and truth.

Jesus offers a paradoxical set of teachings (e.g. the last will be first, we should love our enemies, only someone who is innocent should cast the first stone of criticism) in confronting rigid tradition and religious authoritarianism. His compassion derives from profound empathy and a refusal to accept social division and hierarchy. He presents a vision of how power and authority should be driven by a commitment to community and justice. His vision is of absolute forgiveness but he is not a pushover; at times he is angry and active against injustice. Above all Jesus comes across as holy without being remote; he is mystical in drawing us towards eternity. He is not a moralist telling people what they should do but he puts into practice the way of transforming love.

I believe that Christianity should be defined and judged by its centre (i.e. Jesus Christ) not by its periphery (i.e. the institutional church and its denominations). I find Jesus' call to follow him compulsive not because he taught about being good but because of the integrity between what he taught and the way he lived. I don't believe that anyone is moved to action simply by lectures or sermons but rather by evidence of passion and this is revealed in the love, courage, empathy, humour, wonder and sacrifice of Jesus. Moreover most of us are drawn not by love which is narrow, seeking to possess and control but by love which opens our hearts beyond ourselves and our self-interest, which releases us and sets us free to live fulfilled lives. Jesus was more than simply a teacher of ethics; he preached a radical message of good news based on closeness to the spirit, whom he called God his father; he invited people to be true to the spirit within them; and he lived out his message to the uttermost, eventually dying on a cross. The vision which he proclaimed is one that has taken hold of me and countless others over the years. Sadly human failings within the church which was formed to keep his message alive have distorted and clouded his teachings and his life so that their essence is hidden from view for so many people.

So why do I practise my spirituality in a Christian church?

I believe that religions offer us (as they have over the past 20,000 years) vehicles in scripture, teachings, ritual, and ways of living that help us to experience and enjoy the mysterious, thrilling and deep aspects of human life. At their heart they try to help us to find the sustaining goodness which is at the centre of life and which gives purpose and direction. They all have flaws because they have been constructed by human beings but each in its own way offers myths and models which are ways of imagining ultimate goodness. This does not mean that religion is the only way to satisfy this need; I have tried to show in this book that there are many ways in which we can become more aware of the workings of our soul and more responsive to spirituality. But for me, during my adult life, I have found the essential teachings of Jesus Christ challenging, inspiring and fulfilling, and capable of giving me the experience of ultimate truth.

My understanding of the Christian story is that at the heart of human life is a call to goodness by a spirit that we call God and that if we seek to know God we will experience goodness in our lives. The symbolic story of Jesus Christ provides Christians with a fleshing out of what at its heart goodness is all about. Jesus' teachings, way of living and ultimately his execution as a criminal for trying to challenge the power of the self-interested who set out to dominate others provide a model which is demanding and convincing. The story of Jesus leads us into the presence of God as true goodness and gives Christians a spiritual, moral, political and practical agenda with a radical vision. The Christian story provides me with a credible way of picturing the goodness at the heart of the universe, revealed by a human being whose soul was so filled with God's spirit that he lived his teaching, brought healing and peace, and gave himself for what he believed; after his death many of the men and women who followed him were so convinced that he was still alive that they preached a new religion based on a new way of living through trust in the Christ who offers a reality for those who seek to nurture their soul and respond to the spirit of life. This is a powerful story with a radical truth which inspires me.

Although I have been critical of the baggage added to the Christian story by the theologians of the early church and of the failures of the human institution, the church, which was created to carry this story forward, there is much in the centuries of Christian belief to admire and engage with. Just a few examples will suffice to illustrate this point. People as individuals, inspired by the story of the Christ, have made both amazing personal sacrifices and wonderful world-changing achievements. Some of the most incredible art, architecture and music were created by people filled with a desire to express their faith in the Christian gospel. Christians have produced majestic hymns and glorious liturgies to praise the God of Jesus. Poverty, cruelty and injustice have been challenged and eradicated in Jesus' name. In my view, on balance, much more good than bad has been done and continues to be done by Christians.

So I find myself in fellowship with other Christians and practice my spirituality in a Christian church which I believe takes a modern view of Christianity. Such a view does not see the Bible as absolute and unchanging, a divine product with divine authority to be interpreted literally. Nor does it see Christianity in terms of assenting to archaic doctrine and religious rules in order to earn the reward of life after death. Rather a modern view sees the Bible firstly as an ancient, historical document recording a nation's interactions with its God written by faithful people for the benefit of their own communities; secondly as a source of wisdom, using metaphors to convey the meaning of life rather than factual accuracy; and thirdly as a religious document telling the story of two emerging faiths which is sacred to their adherents. It presents Christianity in terms of how through a close relationship with God we can seek transformation in both our personal and individual life and in the social and political domain.

At the personal level the transformation is about coming to a greater awareness of the spirit in one's daily life. This is expressed in terms of dying to an old way of looking at life and rising to a new way, revealed by Jesus; it is about setting yourself free from the things that hold you back, whatever they may be (self-importance, selfishness, craving for material resources, prejudice, guilt, violence, hatred, etc.) and reconnecting with the things of the spirit (goodness, love, harmony, beauty, peace, joy, fulfilment, etc.). Becoming self-aware is part of the maturing process but it can lead to self-absorption which separates us from God. Jesus teaches that we need to die to our false image of ourselves and be born into an identity filled with the spirit. The process is one of becoming more centred on God and is similar in some ways to the teachings of other religions which urge people to become more aware of their relationship with the spirit and more purposeful in deepening it. The consequence is that we become more loving, more compassionate, more joyful and more at peace.

At the social and political level the transformation is about embracing and pursuing the spiritual claims of fairness and justice, based on Jesus' radical criticism (both in his teaching and his death) of systems. Too often Christians have seen God's justice as being God punishing wrongdoers but even a superficial reading of the Bible reveals that God expects his followers to challenge and eradicate human systems of injustice, whether political, economic, or simply rules of convention. Time and again God is described as passionate about righting injustices such as slavery, exploitation, excessive wealth and poor treatment of the most vulnerable, the widows, orphans, poor and marginalised. He is particularly angry about the religious legitimation of such unjust systems.

Jesus was recognised in his day as uniquely a man of authority and truth; I find the same today in my understanding of him. People came to him for advice and guidance; they respected him not because of any official position or uniform or qualifications but because his truth was compelling and his authority authentic. There is an integrity about him which compels my attention; it will not let me alone; if I turn away, I know that I am denying my own true self. When I look at him I find no anxiety, no exclusivity, no claims to uniqueness and no concern for self. Even though the New Testament picture of Jesus comes to us third-hand, shaped by eye witnesses, early worshippers, and gospel writers, he stands out as someone to be listened to. He inspired trust in others, the kind of trust that led people to give up their jobs and follow him as disciples. He is the one truly free and unique man; he is not someone you can categorise, or classify, or label; he stands above sect, or party, or school of thought; his sole commitment is to the spirit of love and the depth of this commitment frees him from special pleading or rationalisation; it sets him free for truth in the spoken word; in healing and in forgiveness of sins. In him theory and practice were one. By following him I can put my spiritual understanding of life into practice.

Some points to consider

1. Do you identify with the problems of the Christian Church as an institution? Are there other problems of importance to you?
2. Despite the problems the Christian Church has achieved some wonderful things. Can you identify some of them?
3. Where do you stand on the Bible and the Church's handling of Jesus? If you disagree with my analysis can you give some reasons?
4. Where do you stand on the discussion of doctrinal baggage? Are there elements that you would want to preserve? Why? Are there elements other than the ones covered in this chapter that should be discarded?
5. Does my picture of following Jesus make sense for you? Why or why not? Does it challenge and inspire you to respond to his invitation?
6. Do you feel that the final sentence of the chapter is consistent with the rest of the book? Why?

Appendix: A summary of the major religions

This appendix is intended to provide a summary of what are considered to be the current main religions (though some would argue that Buddhism and Confucianism/ Taoism are not really religions). It is deliberately brief and so should not be seen as comprehensive or definitive. The religions covered are Hinduism, Buddhism, Confucianism/Taoism, Judaism, Christianity and Islam. Each religion is analysed under six headings to support the discussion in chapter five. They are:

- a brief history
- beliefs/response to the sacred
- scriptures and theology
- practices, rituals and ceremonies
- the search for higher truth
- structure and organisation.

Before we look at the main religions, let us place them in context by considering the chart on the next page which shows a timeline of about 30,000 years of religious development. Scholars have dated the cave paintings found at Lascaux, Altamira, and other European locations to about 30,000 years ago and believe that they represent the first evidence of religious impulse and the desire to worship. You will see that in such a time-span some of the religions and especially some of the Christian denominations are relatively short-lived.

Millennia/thousands of years before today

| 30 | 29 | 28 | 27 | 26 | 25 | 24 | 23 | 22 | 21 | 20 | 19 | 18 | 17 | 16 | 15 | 14 | 13 | 12 | 11 | 10 | 9 | 8 | 7 | 6 | 5 | 4 | 3 | 2 | 1 |

Earliest religious impulses/Animism

Hinduism

Judaism

Buddhism

Tao/Conf

Christianity

Islam

2009

A very approximate time-line of the development of religions

Centuries/hundreds of years since the birth of Christ

| 1 | 2 | 3 | 4 | 5 | 6 | 7 | 8 | 9 | 10 | 11 | 12 | 13 | 14 | 15 | 16 | 17 | 18 | 19 | 20 |

Early churches

Desert hermits/monasteries

Roman Catholic Church

Benedictines

Orthodox/Eastern Church

Cistercians

Dominicans

Franciscans

Protestantism

Church of England

Puritans, Quakers

Methodism

A very approximate time-line of the development of Christianity

192

HINDUISM

A brief history

Hinduism, the third largest and oldest religion, is believed to date back to 2500BC, though its origins are shrouded in mystery. It has no identifiable founder but emerged over many years from the ancient Vedic civilisation of the Indus Valley, in what is now Pakistan. The majority of the population of India considers itself to be Hindu.

Beliefs/response to the sacred

Over the years Hinduism embraced many diverse beliefs and traditions. Hindus believe that there are many routes to the truth and this pluralism encouraged a multiplicity of sects. The diversity includes polytheism (belief in many gods), panentheism (belief in a god in all of creation and beyond), monotheism (belief in one god) and atheism (belief that there is no god). Hindus can believe in many deities (and there are lots, especially local ones) or in just one (who can be different for different people) or in none. There is no attempt to convert people to belief in a particular god or gods and no idea of heresy. Temples typically have images of many gods within their precincts. There is no sense that other deities are rejected if one is chosen; people are left to respond in their own way to their own spiritual needs.

Scriptures and theology

There is nothing like a creed or a statement of beliefs in Hinduism. The main shared belief, which is a feature also of Buddhism, is that the soul is re-born in successive physical bodies. If one lives a good life, as defined in the ethics/duties of Hinduism, the next re-birth will be into a higher condition; if one lives a bad life, it will be to a lower. At the higher levels it is possible to escape from the cycle of birth, death and rebirth through contemplation, but the ordinary person will mainly be concerned to live a good life in religious terms and to acquire wealth, both of which lead to happiness.

The guide to a good life is found in the sacred texts known as the Vedas, which are the oldest books of any religion and which were written down after being passed on by word of mouth for many centuries. They consist of chants, hymns and mantras to many gods, though the most sacred text, the Rig Veda, points towards belief in one god (monotheism). Later texts known as the Upanishads explain the doctrine of re-birth and teach that the wheel of life revolves around a motionless centre, the supreme, unchanging, eternal reality called Brahman (the sacred), who exists within each individual as their innermost self or soul. When the Hindu becomes fully aware of their soul's identity with Brahman, it is possible to escape from physical existence into spiritual life with the Brahman. This doctrine has tended to create a spiritual elite who place emphasis on asceticism in the form of the ancient tradition of the Sadhu (holy man) bearing physical and mental pain.

The Hindu scriptures refer to *devas* (gods or heavenly beings) who are usually depicted in Hindu culture in human form. They are not the supreme god (*Brahman*) but a reflection of some aspect of *Brahman*. *Brahma* (creator), *Vishnu* (preserver) and *Shiva* (destroyer) are the main gods together with *Rama, Krishna, and Narasimha* (later incarnations of *Vishnu*) and *Shakti* (also called *Durga* or *Kali)*, the mother goddess. In line with the belief in reincarnation, some *devas* come to earth in bodily form and are god-like. The feminine is strongly evidenced in Hinduism; *Lakshmi*, the consort of Vishnu, is one of the most popular goddesses. In the second century BC a theme in Hinduism emerged called *bhakti* (love of a god who is tender and merciful); this is reflected in the most admired of the Hindu classic texts, the *Bhagavad Gita* (Song of the Lord).

Practices, rituals and ceremonies

Given the diversity, one might wonder how the religion is held together. This is mainly achieved through common rituals, often carried out at home since gathering as a group in the temple is less important (apart from during religious festivals) than in other religions. The rituals are mainly to do with purification (washing), prayer, recitation from religious texts, repetition of the name of the god(s), and the offering of food and flowers to icons of the gods at a shrine. There are also sacred rites associated with the main transition points in human life (birth, marriage and death). Pilgrimages are not obligatory but visits to holy sites, including rivers, are undertaken by some Hindus. There are many Hindu holy days but the most popular is the Festival of Lights (*Divali*).

Hindus strongly identify with the animal world and are anxious not to harm any living creature; this has led to the adoption of vegetarianism and to the protection of the cow as sacred. On the other hand, one of the negative aspects of Hinduism, which has only recently been seriously challenged, is the rigid caste system which allocates people at birth into a hierarchy of castes and makes it difficult for people in a lower caste to move to a higher; the worst jobs are reserved for those of the lowest caste.

The search for higher truth

Within Hinduism monks (who can be male or female) are highly respected because of their outward renunciation of selfishness and worldliness. Some live in monasteries, but many are itinerant and there is an expectation that people will offer them hospitality. The monks strive to treat all people with respect and to be indifferent to praise. The ways to achieve higher truth are called *yoga*s and they take four main forms:

- *Bhakti yoga* (the path of love and devotion)
- *Karma yoga* (the path of right action)
- *Rana yoga* (the path of meditation)
- *Thana yoga* (the path of wisdom).

Some schools give priority to *bhakti* but generally the path to be followed by a disciple should include elements of all four.

Structure and organisation

There is no church and there are no priests in Hinduism. There are no denominations though scholars often classify Hindus into groups depending on the main god which they worship as supreme.

BUDDHISM

A brief history

Buddhism started in India around 500BC and had much in common with Hinduism, but it became distinctive when it faded from India and spread across China, Japan and many of the smaller countries of Asia. It is difficult to estimate accurately the number of world-wide adherents, but Buddhism is thought to be the fourth largest religion.

Beliefs/response to the sacred

Among Buddhism's features are an emphasis on gentleness, tolerance and peace, belief in re-birth and a divergence between popular practice and scholarly interpretation. A multiplicity of gods continues to be worshipped at local shrines because they are believed to have power over the good things in life and offer the possibility of escape to paradise.

Many Buddhists do not see Buddhism as a religion because belief in a deity is not a requirement. Some would describe it as a philosophy of spiritual development influenced by its founder; others say that it offers a guide on how to experience greater depth in life. Buddhism sees the idea of the individual as a delusion, our desires and wants as snares which entrap us in the material sphere, and that the way to truth for all people is to escape from the material world. There is no place for God; the pathway to salvation is by human effort alone, though traditional Hindu deities survive in popular practice. The tenor of Buddhist beliefs is pessimistic: life is evil, painful and transitory; it is full of suffering because humans always want more and more and are never satisfied. This is not to suggest that they see humans as evil; they believe humanity is good but has two weaknesses, the desire for individuality and the craving for wealth, success and fame. The concepts of 'I, mine, owning, belonging' are seen as symptoms of belief in a permanent self which is to be promoted and safeguarded; they are the cause of all suffering. Buddhists believe in selflessness, in ceasing to crave and in dissolution of individuality. This leads to perfect serenity, called *nirvana*, which cannot really be described, only experienced. Attempts to describe it use words like the coolness after a fever, perfect peace, freedom and tranquillity, contented non-being. The way to achieve this is through the Buddhist moral code of poverty, chastity and harmlessness and a life of spiritual meditation. Reasoning is rejected as a way to truth.

Scriptures and theology

Buddhism has less diversity than Hinduism; it has a founder and a sacred text of his words (the *Dharma*) written down in Sri Lanka some 400 years after his death (thus being mainly tradition); and it tends to be more ready to seek converts.

Buddha is not the name of the founder of Buddhism; it simply means 'the enlightened one'. (Buddhists believe that there have been many *Buddha*s in the past and that there will be many in the future who will achieve *nirvana*.) His actual name was Gautama, a relatively wealthy Hindu, who was troubled that man is born into the world only to suffer and die. He searched for an answer through asceticism but concluded that this was not the way to become wiser. He wandered on alone until he found the *bodhi* tree of enlightenment and through meditation reached what he called *nirvana* (the extinction of greed, hatred and delusion) through his own efforts. He then taught what he had learned to a group of disciples, who joined him in travelling across north India teaching, befriending the handicapped and outcast. He was not interested in status or social distinctions. He taught a middle way of non-extremism between self-torture and self-indulgence. This teaching is summarised in the Four Noble Truths: that existence involves suffering, that craving is its cause, that suffering can cease with the suppression of desire, and that there is a way to enlightenment through the Noble Eightfold Path, consisting of:

1. right speech	None of these should harm other people (so-called virtuous behaviour).
2. right action	
3. right livelihood	
4. right effort	All of these involve mastery of the mind to become aware of inner reality.
5. right mindfulness	
6. right meditation	
7. right understanding	These are concerned with purification of the mind.
8. right thoughts	

In different branches of Buddhism the first three are expanded into many precepts or rules which govern behaviour (e.g. non-violence, truthfulness, sexual morality, fasting, abstinence from alcohol and drugs), but the key principle in developing the precepts is always pragmatism (is the precept spiritually beneficial?).

Practices, rituals and ceremonies

Ordinary people responded warmly to Gautama's teaching and an order of Buddhist monks was founded, called *Sangha* (the Assembly), to take the movement forward. The monks continue today to pursue the original role of providing a spiritual service to lay people who in turn provide them with a monastery, food and clothing. The monastery acts as the community school, the monks teach and officiate at ceremonies, and many of them become community leaders. The monks are not bound to a particular monastery or to the monastic life; they can leave at any time. In the monastery the monks are able to achieve detachment from the material world and an unworldly frame of mind which fosters contemplation.

Ordinary people keep images of the Buddha at home, and either there or in the pagoda they venerate the Buddha by offering flowers and incense. There may also be images of other deities who are worshipped for their help in worldly matters. The more committed Buddhist will spend one or two hours in meditation each day, as this is regarded as the fundamental route to *nirvana*. There is no formal baptism or reception into membership, no set of rules and no sense of submission for those who wish to commit; they are simply expected to commit to the Buddha's principles of the sacredness of all life, non-violent living and compassion for all. There are many festivals to be celebrated in Buddhism but they tend to vary in timing and content depending on the country in which they are observed. Similarly pilgrimages to Buddhist shrines are encouraged but they are localised.

The search for higher truth

The so-called three jewels of Buddhism are the *Buddha* (i.e. perfect wisdom), the *Dharma* (i.e. the teachings of the *Buddha* concerning behaviour and its consequences) and the *Sangha* (the community of monks or people on their way to enlightenment). Initially Gautama was simply a teacher of the route to perfect wisdom, but later all sorts of miracles were attributed him (e.g. immaculate birth, defeat of the devil after temptation, healing) and he became regarded as divine. His followers regarded him as superior to the other Hindu gods whom they continued to venerate.

Particularly holy monks (male or female) are sometimes regarded as *Bodhisattvas* (people who have reached enlightenment or *nirvana* but remain on earth to continue to teach) and are treated like saints; they are regarded as infinitely compassionate, particularly wise and capable of transferring their spiritual state to their disciples. Sometimes they play a specialised role in a locality and attract cult status.

Structure and organisation

There are several schools of Buddhism, notably Theravada Buddhism and Mahayana Buddhism, which are geographically distinct. Schools which are spread across the world (such as Zen Buddhism) tend to be smaller. The schools exercise a loose control over their member monasteries but there is little hierarchical structure.

CONFUCIANISM AND TAOISM IN CHINA

A brief history

A highly advanced culture was developing in China at the same time as Hinduism was emerging in India. In religious terms, the animistic beliefs that underpinned the Hindu panoply of gods were also to be found in China together with a very strong tradition of ancestor worship. The Chinese kings, later emperors, were believed to be divine and we have archaeological evidence of their servants being buried along with them to continue to serve them in paradise. The king was the chief priest who led ritual gatherings to make sacrifices both to the major deities and to his ancestors. Local shamans did the same for lesser, local deities. The kings believed that they had to pursue virtue in order to remain in favour with heaven; thus religion was an important vehicle for building unity and restraining the behaviour of the ruling classes. There were four key sacrificial rites that the kings/emperors had to lead; to heaven, to earth, to ancestors and to the gods of grain and soil (the last to ensure a good harvest).

Around the time that Gautama was exploring his spirituality, the ancient Chinese religion was starting to collapse as different kingdoms came into conflict and the power of traditional ideas waned. K'ung fu-tsu (Confucius) was a contemporary of Gautama who sought to bring social cohesion to China, not by religious means but through a philosophical and ethical approach which emphasised order, harmony, serenity and decorum.

Beliefs/response to the sacred

He believed in kings/emperors having a mandate from heaven, in ancestor worship, in all people having an appointed place in creation which they should fulfil to the best of their ability and in sacrifice and ritual as unifying forces. He added a code of conduct to these beliefs and promoted education as a way to produce a group of ethical administrators to manage the kingdom/empire.

Confucianism is more a philosophy/moral code than a religion, but it was moulded over the years by religious ideas and is normally practised in the context of a religion.

In particular, elements of Buddhism and Taoism were incorporated into Confucian teaching.

Scriptures and theology

Confucius never wrote anything down but his main disciples elaborated on his ideas. They were gathered in a text called 'The Conversations' or 'Analects' and, and together with six key texts which Confucius edited and two written by his followers, were adopted as the canon during the Han dynasty when examinations started for entry into the civil service. The aims of order, harmony, serenity and decorum were promoted by encouraging a sense of shame on the part of those who fell below the expected standards. A strong sense of duty, benevolence, politeness, formality, loyalty, respect, trustworthiness, calmness and distaste for vulgarity were the marks of the follower of Confucius.

The use of ritual was an important feature of Confucianism, though not in the religious sense. Ritual was seen as a social device to promote politeness and seemly behaviour; it helped people to understand their and other people's role and place in society and their duties towards others. Rituals took the form of protocol and ceremonies which undergirded a highly hierarchical social structure. They were used to promote good governance based on meritocracy. To govern others one has to start by governing oneself, and self-control fosters a sense of calmness at the centre. Such virtuous behaviour was not class-based; Confucius wanted nobility of virtue to replace nobility of blood in order to create social harmony. Such thinking was strengthened by emphasis on piety of children towards their parents (both living and dead), loyalty to family and friends and fair dealing with all people. 'Do as you would be done by' is a key tenet of Confucianism. The perfect gentleman demonstrates morality, filial piety, loyalty and benevolence.

At the time when the canonical texts of Confucianism were being gathered, Taoism had already emerged as a semi-official religion. It drew on Chinese traditions and customs and animistic beliefs but was primarily based on the *Tao Te Ching* (the Way and its Power), an exposition of the mysticism of Lao Tzu, if he actually existed and was not just a figurehead name given to a religious philosophy. Taoism taught that through trance and meditation it is possible to reach a full realisation of the One, the single, unchanging principle which lies behind surface appearances, the unity of which all phenomena are a part. A key component of the teaching is the yin-yang theory of opposites in which wisdom is seen as being in harmony with the rhythms of nature. This leads the believer through meditation (using techniques of asceticism, cleanliness and breathing) to non-interference; union with the Tao is achieved by not trying to achieve it. The Tao is not god and is not worshipped; it is the way to the unifying principle; within Taoism there are gods (from Chinese tradition) who are worshipped in Taoist temples.

Taoist ethics which are expounded in other later books of Taoist wisdom focus on compassion, moderation and humility, with an expectation that followers should draw heavily from energy and action in nature in understanding the world in which they live. The Tao is what keeps the universe in order and balance; it is an invisible power which is present in all things. Man's salvation is to bring his will into harmony with the energy and power of the natural universe.

Practices, rituals and ceremonies

As with many religions, there were elitist and popular versions in Taoism. Some Taoists lived in secluded monasteries and concentrated on meditation. The popular version involved communal worship of many gods and goddesses in seeking to secure good fortune and happiness as well as spiritual improvement; there is a strong element of punishment for sinful behaviour, if it is not repented. Buddhism was successfully brought to China at an early point in its development and influenced and was influenced by Taoism. They assimilated ideas from each other and often coalesced at local level. For example, the practices of Taoism at popular level are very similar to those of Buddhism and vice-versa; people bow before an altar or icons with sticks of incense; they offer sacrifices to the gods or their ancestors in the form of animals, fruit or paper money; they hold street festivals; they make use of fortune tellers; they read, meditate on and recite from the *Tao te Ching*; and they engage in the martial arts for both spiritual and physical benefits. Confucianism was endorsed by the Chinese state as its preferred ethical and philosophical code but a mixture of Confucianism, Buddhism, Taoism and local deities was to be found in Chinese temples. In some countries where there are large Chinese populations, this combination continues.

The search for higher truth

Taoism has similar groups to other religions engaged in reflecting and interpreting its truths. Some are based in monasteries, which have hierarchical structures with an abbot responsible for discipline; others hold respected positions in the community. As their job is to study and interpret the accumulated wisdom in ancient texts, often they are academics, poets or teachers. Among them are mystics who teach the practice of out-of-body meditation.

Structure and organisation

Taoism is organised by a cadre of priests who undergo a long training before they are allowed to conduct rituals in the temples. As the processes of regulating the complementary forces in order to achieve balance are subtle and complex and as healing is often involved, the ceremonies tend to be led by the priest with little congregational involvement.

JUDAISM

A brief history

Judaism is a relatively small world religion in terms of the number of adherents but it needs to be included here because of its huge influence on Christianity and Islam; the three religions share the same roots and are called religions of the road. This means that they see time as linear, not cyclical as in Hinduism and Buddhism; the world had a beginning and will have an end; and the three religions provide an explanation of how humans should respond to this in their lives.

Judaism is one of the oldest religions. It takes as its starting point the covenant between God and Abraham that he would be the leader of a great people if he and the people trusted in God; this covenant was made around 3,000 years ago.

Beliefs/response to the sacred

Its key beliefs are that there is one God, who created the world, entered into a covenant with the Israelites and revealed his law and commandments to Moses. The Jews are descended from the Israelites and they observe God's Law (*Torah*) and follow the guidance of tradition gathered in the *Talmud*.

Judaism is a religion of one people and it permeates the whole of their life; converts not only have to commit to the Jewish faith but also to become a member of the Jewish people with all that that entails. Judaism has an intolerant streak that has carried through into Christianity and Islam. It is strictly monotheistic, deploring, as does Islam, Christianity's worship of Christ and doctrine of the Trinity.

Scriptures and theology

Judaism places its trust completely in the Old Testament as the word of God and is very strict about observation of the Ten Commandments (which are believed to have been handed to Moses by God directly) and of rites/rituals defined in scripture. Over the centuries there have been differences of interpretation of the Holy Scriptures. There is a strong emphasis in Judaism on repentance for sin (which is disobedience of God's laws) and on good behaviour in obedience to God.

The God of Judaism (known as *Yahweh*) is a god of tremendous and terrifying power, displayed in the forces of nature, but also of mercy and benevolence – a god of discipline but also of love. Jewish religious ideas are developed in the words and actions of the great heroes of the faith such as Moses, the prophets and King David; monotheism fostered the development of a clear moral code and formed the basis for national unity. Jerusalem was seen as God's chosen home and King Solomon built a magnificent temple to be the spiritual centre of the world. Life is seen as good if lived in accordance with God's laws; there is no place for asceticism in Judaism. However, the people of Israel are described in the Old Testament as continually wandering away from *Yahweh* in terms of worship and behaviour and have to be called back by the prophets, who warn of dire consequences for those who abandon their faith. The consequences are largely seen in terms of being over-run and sent into slavery by opposing nations.

It was in the course of some of the lengthy periods when the Jews were in captivity or had been over-run that they were influenced by the ideas of Zoroastrianism in Persia and Greek philosophy in the Hellenistic empire. The idea of a saviour who would come to save them (they called the saviour the Messiah) emerged during this time. Other key beliefs such as the resurrection of the dead, the ongoing battle between good and evil, the last judgement, heaven and hell and the future perfection of the world became prominent at least among some sects.

Eventually their country was occupied by Rome and in 70AD Jerusalem was laid waste; as a result the Jews were scattered. Religious leadership passed from the scribes and Pharisees, who had run things from Jerusalem, to the local rabbis who were not priests but teachers. Dispersal could have led to the disappearance of Judaism but a faithful remnant led by the rabbis preserved the faith and maintained observance of the laws and customs.

Practices, rituals and ceremonies

Some 500 years after the destruction of Jerusalem, the *Talmud* (a collection of sermons, moral tales, legends and popular stories) was written and became the basis for Jewish devotions, especially at home, with stress on thanksgiving, purification, clean food, self-control, personal holiness, regular prayer (in the morning, afternoon and evening), special religious clothing (such as skull cap, prayer shawls), and dietary constraints. The Sabbath holy day of rest (requiring observance of traditional practice), the three key festivals of pilgrimage when the Israelites travelled to Jerusalem to offer sacrifices in the Temple (Passover, commemorating the escape from slavery in Egypt, Pentecost, commemorating the revelation of the Law to Moses, and Tabernacles, commemorating the forty years of wandering in the wilderness prior to reaching the promised land) and the high holy days of Remembrance (the Jewish New Year) and Atonement (a solemn day of fasting and prayer for forgiveness of sins) continued to be observed, together with a number of more minor festivals. In addition, Jews have placed importance on the observation of rites of passage such as circumcision of boys eight days after birth, passage from adolescence to adulthood (*bar-mitzvah* for boys, *bat-mitzvah* for girls), marriage and death/mourning.

These rituals are the essence of Judaism, bringing regularly to mind the Torah and the Talmud; the neglect of such rituals would lead to the death of Judaism.

Jews worship God in synagogues, simple rectangular buildings oriented towards Jerusalem, with the sign of David (crossed triangles) over the entrance. The synagogues have rooms set aside for prayer, study and teaching but there are no pictures or images and so the building may seem austere. In the worship area will be found an ark in which the scrolls of the Law are kept, and an elevated platform on which the reader of the Law stands when reading, a pulpit or lectern facing the ark from which prayers are led and talks are given, and an eternal light as a reminder of the constantly lit lamp of the Temple in Jerusalem. The spiritual leaders of the Jewish community are the rabbis and they are supported by prayer leaders, readers of the Law and a chant leader. The men of Israel (males over 13) sit with the rabbi in the body of the synagogue whilst the women and children watch from the gallery.

The search for higher truth

The Jewish faith has relatively little time for continuing to search; it believes that it is the one true faith and has been fully revealed. Thus its emphases are on action, family and community i.e. putting God's commandments into practice in a close family setting and preserving the community dimension. The spiritual elite in Judaism devote themselves to meditation on the Torah.

Structure and organisation

Many Jews suffered persecution over the centuries at the hands of the Christians because of their role in the crucifixion of Christ but Jewish intellectual life continued to flourish. The rabbis played a key role in maintaining the integrity of the faith over the years and the close family/community focus provided continuity. The influence of western ideas led to a Reform movement in the nineteenth century and this in turn led traditionalists into a firmer orthodoxy, with conservatives falling in between. These three groups continue to exist, most of the Reform synagogues being in the USA, and most of the orthodox being in Israel, but a number of other sub-groups with particular interests have been formed more recently. The Zionist movement which began to seek an Israeli state in the late nineteenth century had little influence until the Nazi massacres of Jews in the holocaust which led to a surge in world opinion in favour of the state of Israel which was created in 1948.

CHRISTIANITY

A brief history

Christianity is the world's largest religion, with one in four of the world's population as adherents; the number of adherents is increasing in the developing world as it declines in the western world. Christianity began as an offshoot of Judaism and accepts the Hebrew Bible as part of its holy scriptures; it is described as an Abrahamic religion because, with Judaism and Islam, it traces its origins back to God's covenant with Abraham. It remained quite small, having been dismissed by the Jews and others as disreputable and unbelievable, until it was adopted for political reasons by the Roman empire in the fourth century AD and became the state religion, thus being taken to all countries under Roman domination. Sadly in the eleventh century the differences in doctrine between the western (Rome-based) and eastern (Byzantium-based) churches were too difficult to reconcile and the major schism, as it has come to be known, took place when the eastern church refused to accept the authority of the Pope. This was the first of many divisions.

Beliefs/response to the sacred

Despite the complexity of the doctrines that developed, Christianity proved very attractive, perhaps as a result of the picture of goodness, love and strength portrayed in the Gospel pictures of Jesus and the manner and meaning of his death. The idea of God coming to live on earth is strikingly unique even though the notion of a saviour who suffers rejection, torture and execution is more common in ancient mythology.

Jesus is believed to be the Messiah or Son of God; the name Christ conveys this. His coming was prophesied in the Old Testament, but when he came he interpreted the role of Messiah very differently from his contemporaries. He took up a theme in the prophecies recorded in the Book of Isaiah of the Messiah as a suffering servant and taught his disciples that the Son of God must suffer temptation, pain, conflict, torture and death before being raised to return to his Father God. This was interpreted by the early church into a belief that through Jesus' death and resurrection sinful human beings can be reconciled with God and offered the possibility of eternal life. Jesus was seen to be sinless and to have defeated death and the worst that evil could throw at human beings. As a result God raised him from death. This is the cornerstone of the Christian faith; without it God is seen to be a sadistic tyrant who sent his son to death on a cross and was powerless to intervene. Christians assert that God has power over life and death and can give humans the opportunity to enter eternal life after death. Thus salvation is believed to be an unmerited gift of God to human beings who through faith in Jesus can be saved from sin and death. There are many different interpretations of salvation in the many sects of Christianity.

Scriptures and theology

Christianity is by far the most complicated religion in terms of divisions and doctrines. There is not space in this short summary to cover all aspects of a faith which has been so influential in the west, but more is said in the final chapter.

Christianity's moral code, drawing on Judaism, is straightforward and relatively easy to understand. Jesus comes as the Messiah, bridging the gap between God and human beings, and on the face of it offers people love, understanding, forgiveness, survival of death and eternal life in heaven. These simple ideas, when they were challenged over the centuries, were made amazingly complicated by heavy theology (unheard of in most religions) based on the Old and New Testaments. Very little is known about Jesus historically; he wrote nothing; the gospels that describe his life were written for missionary purposes, not as historical texts. But he was undoubtedly a great moral teacher; he taught in simple but profound ways; he is authoritative, mysterious, challenging; he had supernatural skills; and he was close to the God whom he called his father. The resurrection is the key event; if it had not happened we would never have heard of Jesus; but his frightened and uneducated disciples were convinced by what we call the resurrection that he was alive, despite having been executed a short while before, so much so that they risked life and limb to tell people what they had seen and heard. Shortly after his death, one of the fiercest opponents of the new faith, Saul of Tarsus, who was persecuting Christians with great fervour, was convinced by a vision of Jesus that he was alive and available to him. Saul changed his name to Paul and became the person who more than anyone else defined the Christian faith through his letters.

Another early development, which became a source of conflict with the other Abrahamic religions, was the doctrine of the Holy Trinity. This was a mechanism to give equal status to God the Father, God the Son, and God the Holy Spirit which the early church had seen as three persons acting in consort but in different ways. This was seen by people outside the Christian Church as a move away from monotheism.

Practices, rituals and ceremonies

Christian worship takes place at home or in church and takes very diverse forms. Usually corporate worship involves the singing of hymns, reading of scripture, some form of exhortation to the faithful, and prayer (including the saying of the Lord's Prayer which is based on a prayer which Jesus taught). Beyond that it can vary enormously in content, style, language, setting and doctrinal emphases. With regard to ritual practice, Christians refer to sacraments instituted by Jesus that mediate God's presence. There are disagreements about the number of sacraments seen as central to the church's worship, but most denominations/ sects do observe the sacraments of Baptism and Eucharist. Baptism is a sacrament of entry into the church and Eucharist is a commemoration of the last evening of Jesus' life when he shared bread and wine with his disciples and asked them to continue to do so in memory of him. Once again there are many different interpretations of what is happening in baptism and the Eucharist. Other sacraments observed by some churches include confirmation (or receiving new believers into membership), ordination of presbyters/ priests, marriage, anointing the sick, and confession. As in other religions, the high points of human life are marked with Christian rituals.

The major Christian festivals have found their way into the western calendar. The most important are Christmas when Christ's birth is celebrated and Easter when the events of the crucifixion and resurrection are commemorated and celebrated. These are high points for the believer and times of festivity for non-believers as well. There are many other festivals in the Christian calendar and some countries mark every day in the year as a saint's day.

The search for higher truth

Throughout its history, leading thinkers in the Christian Church have written at length about ways of coming close to God. It is a constant focus of thought and there is not space here to do justice to the ideas save to say that meditation and mysticism have become more important Christian practices, perhaps as a result of greater knowledge of practices in other religions.

Structure and organisation

As the church grew, there were many doctrinal arguments which led to deep divisions. The Roman empire could not afford to have a divided state religion and so heads were knocked together and a definitive set of beliefs was written by the institutional church. Those who could not accept them were declared heretics and excommunicated. This has happened throughout the history of what has turned out to be at times a very intolerant institution, despite believing in the most tolerant, inclusive and caring person who has probably ever lived. The Roman church became corrupt and violent in maintaining its power (e.g. crusades, inquisitions, indulgences, infallible Popes, ruthless missionary ventures which left hundreds of thousands killed, and failure to challenge injustice all over the world). As a result many times over the years people have protested and called for change; usually they were simply removed/obliterated; occasionally they led change (e.g. the monastic movement, the Protestant Reformation, the evangelical revival and the existence of a large number of sects).

Despite all of this the simple message of Jesus has won large numbers of individuals to amazing acts of service, commitment, love and courage. Ecumenism, led by the Protestants, is trying to bring the church together again but major doctrinal disagreements continue (e.g. over original sin, women priests, abortion, meaning of the mass, nature of Jesus, understanding of the Trinity, deification, etc.). The deep divisions of attitude, temperament and tradition do not augur well for the future of Christianity in the west.

Because Christianity is very large and has had a long time to get organised, it is highly structured with a strong, male-dominated hierarchy. Every denomination does things differently but it is worth noting that a considerable number of professional people are employed by the church (as priests, ministers, bishops etc) in order to maintain its functioning. In most of the churches, they hold the positions of power.

ISLAM

A brief history

Islam is the youngest of the major religions, dating from around 600AD, and has the second (after Christianity) largest number of adherents across the world. The key foundation of the religion is the *Qur'an* (word of God) revealed to Muhammad. Muhammad came from a relatively poor, obscure background but from an early age spent a lot of time in meditation and prayer. He was familiar with the teachings of Judaism and Christianity and believed their God to be the same as *Allah*. Around the age of 40 he had a vision that he was called as a prophet to bring people back to worship of the true God. He won a few converts in Mecca but many more in Medina where he became the leader of the community. Muhammad showed a considerable gift of leadership, operating spiritually in the mould of an Old Testament prophet. He taught that Abraham and Ishmael were Muslims, expelled the Jews from Medina and claimed that the Arabs were God's standard-bearers rather than the Jews. He formed a Muslim state in Medina and became the religious as well as political leader. He waged holy wars on his neighbours in order to expand Medina's territory but proclaimed that Muslims should not fight against one another, thereby focusing their attention on the infidels. After eight years his forces took Mecca without a struggle, destroying all idols and preserving the *Ka'ba* (a black stone believed to have been given to Abraham by Gabriel, now sited in the courtyard of the Great Mosque) which was dedicated to *Allah* and made an object of pilgrimage. He then returned to Medina and shortly afterwards died. Muhammad was insistent during his life that he was not divine and had no miraculous powers, despite his visions and ecstatic trances during which his words were recorded and make up the *Qur'an*. He saw himself as the last in the line of great prophets stretching from Moses to Jesus, but after his death his followers started to worship him as divine.

Beliefs/response to the sacred

Islam means 'submission to the will of God'; Muslim means 'one who submits'. Its simple creed (*tawhid*) is "There is no god but God and Muhammad is God's messenger" and it shares the same God (called *Allah*) as Judaism and Christianity. The Old Testament prophets and Jesus are respected as forerunners of Muhammad but Muslims believe that Muhammad came to correct the erroneous ideas of Jews and Christians. For example, they do not believe that the Jews are God's chosen people, do not accept Jewish law, do not believe that Jesus is the Son of God (this is seen as contradicting monotheism) and do not see God as being in a fatherly relationship with human beings.

Scriptures and theology

The Qu'ran was finalised in the twenty years after Muhammad's death and so there is a unique connection between the founder of Islam and its holy book. It is written in Arabic and scholars consider it to have inspiring beauty and forcefulness. Muslims regard the sacred *Qur'an* as infallible, capable of providing protection against disease and misfortune; it is learned by heart as a child and forms the basis for Muslim education. In consequence Islam remains closer to the teachings of its founder than almost all other religions. The main emphasis of the *Qur'an* is on the overwhelming power and majesty of God, who is responsible for all good and evil in the world. A key belief is in the existence of angels who are God's messengers who communicate his will to humans. The angels look after the believer in battle, keep a record of his deeds, care for his soul in death and intercede for the believer on the day of judgement.

In the fullness of time God will judge the way people have lived and the righteous will go to paradise (a place of great beauty and serenity where erotic pleasures are assured) and unbelievers will descend to the agonies of hell. Death is regarded not as something to be feared but as the gateway to paradise for the faithful. The *Qur'an* lacks the preoccupation with sin and sex which featured in early Christianity. There is no concept of original sin. Murder, theft, adultery, pork, wine and gambling are all forbidden. Justice, fair dealing, kind treatment of women, slaves and orphans, generosity to the poor, respect for parents and hospitality for the traveller are all promoted. The Qur'an is backed up by tradition (*hadith*) which goes back to Muhammad's time and provides detailed rules and regulations which form the basis for *Shar'ia* law which is believed to apply to all mankind and consists of rulings that touch on virtually all aspects of life. There has been a tendency towards inflexibility and conservatism in interpreting both the *Qur'an* and the *Hadith*.

Practices, rituals and ceremonies

The five pillars of Islam, which are required of all adherents, are recitation of the creed (*shahadah*), praying five times each day facing Mecca (*salah*), giving to charity (*zakat*), fasting (*sawm*) (mainly during the month of Ramadan) and making a pilgrimage to Mecca (*hajj*) at least once in one's life-time. These requirements provide collective self-discipline among the faithful, as there is no priesthood (the local *imam*s are teachers rather than priests and the faithful are all equal before God), no concept of church (society as a whole is the institutional form), no music or singing of hymns, no rituals and no images in the buildings called mosques where they study and worship communally. In each mosque there is a semi-circular recess (*mihrab*) which shows the direction of Mecca for the praying faithful. Community prayers take place on Fridays (the Muslim Sabbath) at the mosque; they are preceded by a washing ritual of purification. Prayers can be said anywhere but the communal prayer on Fridays is an important element of the faith. Although women can enter the mosque, they usually make their prayers at home. There is no idea of God coming close to or being active within the individual.

There are several festivals and holy days in Islam but the key one is Eid ul Fitr which marks the end of Ramadan and is an occasion of considerable celebration and joy.

Muslims are required by the *Qur'an* to propagate their faith through *jihad* (striving) in God's name and this has included holy wars. Within one hundred years of Muhammad's death the Muslims ruled an area larger than the Roman empire at its peak. In these countries people were allowed to retain their previous religion, but not proselytise, provided they paid a tax. The speed and extent of the growth of the Muslim empire led to infighting among Muhammad's family and friends.

The search for higher truth

The mystical wing of Islam is called Sufism and it has many parallels with the desert fathers within Christianity and the holy men of Hinduism and Buddhism. The Sufis believe that union with God is possible, without sharing identity, and their meditative and mystical spirituality led to the formation of monasteries in which the sheikh has absolute power over the monks as the abbot does in other religions. Some Sufis have become regarded as saints and supernatural/magical powers have been claimed for them.

Structure and organisation

There are many sects and schools within Islam. They tend to be classified in three groups: the modernisers who wish to take on some Western and scientific ideas; the conservatives who wish to retain the ancient traditions; and the radical/fanatical nationalists who are seeking Muslim domination in countries where they have a majority. Despite the divisions, Muslims across the world see their faith as uniting them and providing an essential element of their identity.

<u>OTHER SMALLER RELIGIONS</u>

There is insufficient space to cover all religions but before finishing this Appendix we will consider three of the smaller ones which have influenced the main ones which we have covered.

Jainism

Jainism is an ancient Indian religion that influenced the development of Hinduism and Buddhism. It teaches the need to care for all living things because they (animals and plants, as well as humans) have souls, which are of equal value; Jains are strict vegetarians and try to minimise their use of the world's resources. Jainism also teaches the possibility of escape from the cycle of birth, death and rebirth by eliminating all karma from the soul; Jains believe that there are no gods or spiritual beings that will help humans to achieve this; rather the human must seek his or her own solution through non-violence, non-attachment to possessions, not lying, not stealing, and sexual restraint. Jainism has no priests, but there are many monks and nuns, who lead strict and ascetic lives. Most Jains today are in India; there are around four million across the world.

Sikhism

There are about 20 million Sikhs in the world, mainly in the Punjab. Sikhism was founded in the sixteenth century by Guru Nanak and is based largely on his teachings. He stressed the importance of action rather than ritual, and taught the need to keep God in the heart and mind at all times as well as being honest, treating people fairly, being generous to the disadvantaged and serving others. Sikhism is strongly based in the community of believers, called the Khalsa, who make decisions based on their founder's principles.

Zoroastrianism

Zoroastrianism is probably the oldest monotheistic religion, having been founded by Zoroaster (or Zarathustra) around 3,500 years ago. For a thousand years it was the official religion of Persia. Zoroastrians believe in one god, the creator of the world, whose light and wisdom they represent as fire. They had a strong influence on Judaism during the period of the Jewish exile, especially in introducing ideas such as a saviour who would bring salvation, resurrection of the dead, the battle between good and evil, the last judgement, heaven and hell and the future perfection of the world.

[The contents of this Appendix are based on a search of several websites. The main ones were Wikipedia (en. wikipedia.org/wiki/Hinduism etc.) and the religion section of the BBC website (www.bbc.co.uk/religion/religions), but many of the sites hyper-linked from these were also explored. If you would like to follow up this brief summary, both sites will provide useful starting points.]

Acknowledgements and ideas for further study

This book reflects my developing thinking over about thirty years. During that period I have read many books both as a requirement of the Methodist Church basic and advanced local preaching examinations and I have talked to many people. In teaching the Christian faith and in preaching sermons I have read widely and engaged in some challenging discussions. So, many of the ideas for the content of this book have come from a mix of now unidentifiable sources.

When I felt a desire to write about spirituality, I decided to take a postgraduate course in the area to check and challenge my ideas. This involved a lot of reading, most of which confirmed my opinions (or perhaps I chose only to read books which were of this kind!). I found that there were several academic books that already did what I had planned, and so there was no point in repeating them. So I decided to try to write a personal account of my discovery of spirituality. As it is not an academic book, the references are few but if any reader wishes to go into greater detail, I would recommend the following books:

For a deeper insight into spirituality: Diarmuid O'Murchu, "Reclaiming spirituality" (Gill & MacMillan, Dublin, 1997).

For a practical discussion of the soul in today's world: any recent book by Thomas Moore, such as "The Soul's Religion" (HarperCollins, New York, 2002).

For ideas about spiritual living: any recent book by Ronald Rolheiser such as "Seeking Spirituality" (Hodder & Stoughton, London, 1998).

For an exploration of how religions share similar spiritual ideas: Brian Pierce, "We walk the way together" (Orbis Books, New York, 2005).

For a modern interpretation of Christianity: any recent book by John Selby Spong or Marcus Borg, especially the latter's "The Heart of Christianity" (HarperCollins, New York, 2004).

But if you do not care for reading academic books, you may prefer to read a novel or see a film that illustrates a spiritual understanding of life. Here are ten examples of each, which I have found enjoyable and rewarding. Try them.

Novels:

- Mitch Alborn, "For one more day", Sphere, 2006
- Muriel Barbery, "The Elegance of the Hedgehog", Gallic Books, 2008
- Paul Coelho, "The Alchemist", Harper Collins, 1995
- Khaled Hosseini, "A Thousand Splendid Suns", Bloomsbury Publishing, 2004
- Yann Martel, "Life of Pi", Canongate, 2003
- Audrey Nifnegger, "The Time Traveller's Wife", Vintage, 2004
- Mary-Ann Schaffer and Annie Barrows, "The Guernsey Literary and Potato Peel Pie Society", Bloomsbury Publishing, 2009
- Alice Seebold, "The Lovely Bones", Picador, 2002

- John Steinbeck. "The Pearl", Penguin, 2001
- Marcus Zusak, "The Book Thief", Black Swan, 2008

Films on DVD

- "Babette's Feast", MGM, 2004
- "Central Station", Miramax, Walt Disney, 2004
- "Chocolat", Walt Disney, 2001
- "Pay it forward", Warner Bros, 2000
- "Philadelphia", Sony, 1993
- "Schindler's List", Universal, 2006
- "The Boy in the Striped Pyjamas", Miramax, 2008
- "The Chorus", Pathe, 2005
- "The Shawshank Redemption", Castle Rock, 1994
- "Whale Rider", Icon, 2002

Finally, I would especially like to thank the following people who read the first draft and offered very helpful comments and advice: David Bidnell, Jan Hicks, Jenny Lee, Nigel Nixon and Sheila Lee.

Lightning Source UK Ltd.
Milton Keynes UK
04 March 2011
168702UK00001B/3/P